4D HYPL....

A Cultural Toolkit for the Open-Source City

Profile
No 245

ARCHITECTURAL DESIGN
January/February 2017

@BC

Guest-Edited by
LUCY BULLIVANT

About the
Guest-Editor

Lucy Bullivant

05

Introduction
The Hyperlocal

Less Smart City, More
Shared Social Value

Lucy Bullivant

06

Practices of
the Minimum
Viable Utopia

Adam Greenfield

16

The
Posthuman
City

Imminent Urban Commons

Alejandro Zaera-Polo

26

AZPML,
Seun Sangga
arcade,
Seoul, South
Korea, 2015

Projective
Empowerment

Co-creative Sustainable
Design Processes

Bess Krietemeyer

36

Biodigital
Design
Workflows

ecoLogicStudio's Solana
Open Aviary in Ulcinj,
Montenegro

Claudia Pasquero
and Marco Poletto

44

ecoLogicStudio,
Solana Open Aviary,
Ulcinj, Montenegro,
2016

The
Hackable City

Citymaking in
a Platform Society

Martijn de Waal,
Michiel de Lange
and Matthijs Bouw

50

From Citizen
Participation to
Real Ownership

Driving the Regeneration
of Amsterdam's Amstel3
District

Saskia Beer

58

Imagined
Community
and Networked
Hyperlocal
Publics

John Bingham-Hall

64

ISSN 0003-8504
ISBN 978-1119-097129

Guest-Edited by **Lucy Bullivant**

Conflict Urbanism, Aleppo

Mapping Urban Damage

Laura Kurgan

72

Suburban Resonance in Segrate, Milan

The Language of Locative Media in Defining Urban Sensitivity

Raffaele Pe

78

VoiceOver

Citizen Empowerment Through Cultural Infrastructure

Usman Haque

86

Umbrellium,
VoiceOver,
Horden, County
Durham, 2016

Digital Neighourhoods

Hyperlocal Village Hubs in Rural Communities

Katharine Willis

92

Sentiment Architectures as Vehicles for Participation

Moritz Behrens

98

Moritz Behrens
and Konstantinos
Mavromichalis,
Sentiment Cocoon,
Arup offices,
London, 2015

△ 4D Hyperlocal Would Like to Use Your Current Location

Will Gowland and Samantha Lee

104

The Image of a Data City

Studying the Hyperlocal with Social Media

Lev Manovich and Agustin Indaco

110

Check-In

Foursquare and the Rich Annotated Topology of Citizen-Generated Hyperlocal Data

José Luis de Vicente

118

Counterpoint Tell 'Em They're Dreamin'

Mark Burry

126

Contributors

134

3

Editorial Offices
John Wiley & Sons
9600 Garsington Road
Oxford
OX4 2DQ

T +44 (0)1865 776868

Consultant Editor
Helen Castle

Managing Editor
Caroline Ellerby
Caroline Ellerby Publishing

Freelance Contributing Editor
Abigail Grater

Publisher
Paul Sayer

Art Direction + Design
CHK Design:
Christian Küsters
Christos Kontogeorgos

Production Editor
Elizabeth Gongde

Prepress
Artmedia, London

Printed in Italy by Printer
Trento Srl

Front cover: Bess
Krietemeyer, Amber
Bartosh and Lorne
Covington/NOIRFLUX,
Computational hybrid-
reality model, Interactive
Design and Visualization
Lab (IDVL), Syracuse
Center of Excellence,
Syracuse University,
New York, 2016. © Lorne
Covington/NOIRFLUX
2016

Inside front cover:
Umbrellium, VoiceOver,
Horden, County
Durham, 2016. © Richard
Kenworthy

01/2017

ARCHITECTURAL DESIGN

January/February
2017

Profile No.
245

Disclaimer
The Publisher and Editors cannot be held responsible
for errors or any consequences arising from the use
of information contained in this journal; the views and
opinions expressed do not necessarily reflect those of
the Publisher and Editors, neither does the publication
of advertisements constitute any endorsement by
the Publisher and Editors of the products advertised.

Journal Customer Services
For ordering information,
claims and any enquiry
concerning your journal
subscription please go to
www.wileycustomerhelp
.com/ask or contact your
nearest office.

Americas
E: cs-journals@wiley.com
T: +1 781 388 8598 or
+1 800 835 6770 (toll free
in the USA & Canada)

**Europe, Middle East
and Africa**
E: cs-journals@wiley.com
T: +44 (0)1865 778315

Asia Pacific
E: cs-journals@wiley.com
T: +65 6511 8000

Japan (for Japanese-
speaking support)
E: cs-japan@wiley.com
T: +65 6511 8010 or 005 316
50 480 (toll-free)

Visit our Online Customer
Help available in 7 languages
at www.wileycustomerhelp
.com/ask

Print ISSN: 0003-8504
Online ISSN: 1554-2769

Prices are for six issues
and include postage and
handling charges. Individual-
rate subscriptions must be
paid by personal cheque or
credit card. Individual-rate
subscriptions may not be
resold or used as library
copies.

All prices are subject to
change without notice.

Identification Statement
Periodicals Postage paid
at Rahway, NJ 07065.
Air freight and mailing in
the USA by Mercury Media
Processing, 1850 Elizabeth
Avenue, Suite C, Rahway,
NJ 07065, USA.

USA Postmaster
Please send address changes
to *Architectural Design*,
John Wiley & Sons Inc.,
c/o The Sheridan Press,
PO Box 465, Hanover,
PA 17331, USA.

Rights and Permissions
Requests to the Publisher
should be addressed to:
Permissions Department
John Wiley & Sons Ltd
The Atrium
Southern Gate
Chichester
West Sussex PO19 8SQ
UK

F: +44 (0)1243 770 620
E: Permissions@wiley.com

All Rights Reserved. No
part of this publication
may be reproduced, stored
in a retrieval system or
transmitted in any form or
by any means, electronic,
mechanical, photocopying,
recording, scanning or
otherwise, except under
the terms of the Copyright,
Designs and Patents Act
1988 or under the terms
of a licence issued by the
Copyright Licensing Agency
Ltd, 90 Tottenham Court
Road, London W1T 4LP, UK,
without the permission in
writing of the Publisher.

Subscribe to ⟁
⟁ is published bimonthly
and is available to purchase
on both a subscription basis
and as individual volumes
at the following prices.

Prices
Individual copies:
£24.99 / US$39.95
Individual issues on
⟁ App for iPad:
£9.99 / US$13.99
Mailing fees for print
may apply

Annual Subscription Rates
Student: £84 / US$129
print only
Personal: £128 / US$201
print and iPad access
Institutional: £275 / US$516
print or online
Institutional: £330 / US$620
combined print and online
6-issue subscription on
⟁ App for iPad: £44.99 /
US$64.99

Lucy Bullivant PhD Hon FRIBA is a cultural historian, award-winning author, a Built Environment Expert (BEE) for Design Council Cabe, London, and founder and Creative Director of Urbanista.org, a webzine on liveable urbanism. In 2010 she was elected an Honorary Fellow of the Royal Institute of British Architects (RIBA) for her services to architectural culture globally, and she received her PhD by Prior Output for 'From Masterplanning to Adaptive Planning: Understanding the Contemporary Tools and Processes for Civic Urban Order' from the Sir John Cass School of Art, Architecture and Design at London Metropolitan University in 2015. She was a professor of urban design history and theory for Syracuse University (2013–14), and a jury member for ArchMarathon, Milan (2014 and 2015–16). She has been a member of the Scientific and Steering Committee, Institut pour la Ville en Mouvement, Paris since 2011 and of the Comité Technique at FRAC, Orléans since 2010.

Lucy's research topics include alternative masterplanning and adaptive frameworks; relational urbanism and social equity in the formal and informal city; hyperlocal digital–physical strategies; and urban imaginaries. She is the guest-editor of the △ issues *4dspace: Interactive Architecture* (Jan/Feb 2005) and *4dsocial: Interactive Design Environments* (July/August 2007). In this issue she explores the different manifestations and implications of emerging hyperlocal modes of design using geolocal technologies. This ecology of adaptable tools, platforms and networks is more than a domain of design specialists; it facilitates a wider engagement in local contexts, with projects and strategies promoting a more inclusive commons based on distributed participatory systems – a cultural toolkit for open-source urbanism.

She has curated exhibitions including 'Remake – We Make: Frameworks for Social and Cultural Exchange' for the Bi-City Biennale of Urbanism\Architecture in Shenzhen (2015); 'Urbanistas: Women Innovators in Architecture, Urban and Landscape Design' for Roca London Gallery (2015); 'Space Invaders', with Pedro Gadanho, for the British Council (2001–3); 'Kid Size: The Material World of Childhood', co-curated with the Vitra Design Museum (1997–2005); and 'The Near and the Far: Fixed and in Flux', the British exhibition at the XIX Triennale di Milano (1996), supported by the UK government.

Her books include *Masterplanning Futures* (Routledge, 2012), which was Book of the Year at the Urban Design Awards, 2014; *Recoded City: Co-Creating Urban Futures* (Routledge, 2015), on participatory placemaking and co-authored with Thomas Ermacora; *New Arcadians: Emerging UK Architects* (Merrell, 2012); *Responsive Environments: Architecture, Art and Design* (V&A Contemporary, 2006); and *Anglo Files: UK Architecture's Rising Generation* (Thames & Hudson, 2005). Lucy is an editor of publications on aspects of the relationship between architecture, design, digital technology and society, including *bio_Tallinn* (Tallinn Biennale of Architecture, 2017) and *Sustainable Urbanism* (University of Qatar, 2016). Her investigative journalism has been published in the Cities and International Development sections of *The Guardian*, and she has been writing features for leading specialist architecture and design media since 1987, including *Domus, Volume, Harvard Design Magazine, Architectural Review, Architecture Today, A+U, Uncube, Platform, Indesign, Habitus, The Architect's Newspaper, Metropolis* and *The Plan*.

The Hyperlo

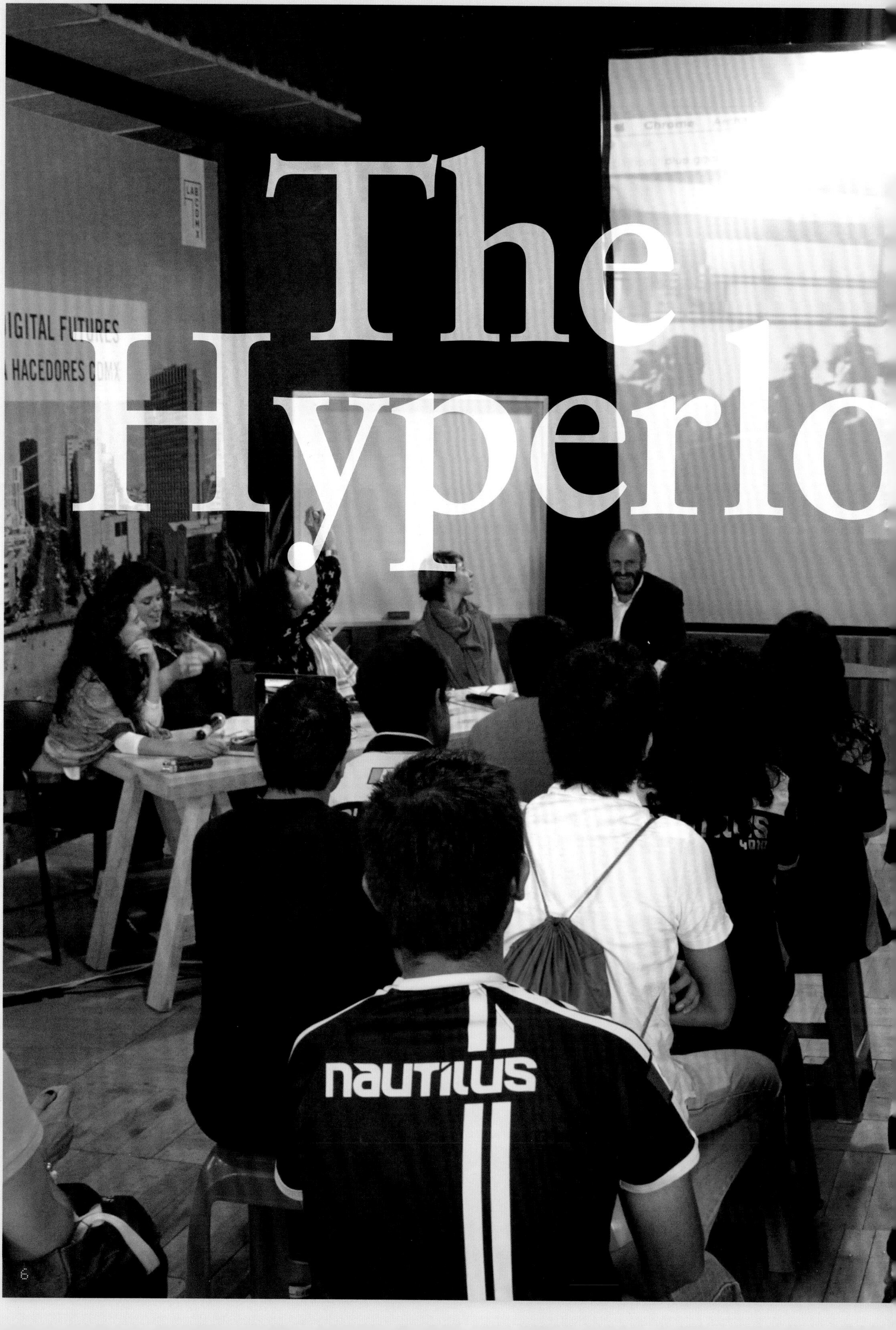

INTRODUCTION

LUCY BULLIVANT

V&A Digital Programmes, the British Council and Laboratorio para la Ciudad, Digital Futures UKMX, Mexico City and Dundee, 2015

The project brought together citizens from communities in Mexico City and Dundee in a series of prototyping labs and hackathons in both locations. Participants used open tools such as a Periscope live-streaming link for cross-cultural discussions on issues such as the environment, climate, open data, waste and sustainability.

Less Smart City, More Shared Social Value

The hyperlocal is indicative of a particular mindset. Enabled by digital tools and open-source activities, it is a social ecology due to the fact that it is underpinned by a belief that on-the-ground engagement and shared resources are of fundamental benefit to the evolution of communities and cities. The challenges of urbanisation globally since the 1960s, and the social myopia of many top-down urban developments, have encouraged alternative models to be forged as part of a wider commitment to cultural self-determination.

Advances in tech culture of the last decade or so have opened up many potent possibilities for individuals and groups to co-create and apply their own tools to urban needs. This issue of D explores the plural characteristics, significance and uses of the hyperlocal as an emerging form of digitally facilitated – or four-dimensional – design. These are taking shape at a time of many civic-tech innovations, ranging from municipal governments opening up their data to improve quality of life (and making better use of it themselves), helping to break down silos and forge dialogues between different stakeholders, to driverless trains with the potential to remove human error.

The hyperlocal's community value is growing in areas ranging from medicine to urban design, environmental resources to information sharing. As a field of actions and distributed capacities for social infrastructure it is greatly at variance with the narrow vision of industry-driven, smart-city urban development. The repertoire of the latter deploys Internet of Things sensors and actuators to collect, in an unconstrained way, data about energy and transport that can be analysed to efficiently manage complex urban systems. Rather than being a generic 'tech kit', the hyperlocal's emerging, alternative toolsets respond to specific commons (public localities). Their value is incalculable in contexts where digital connections are not ubiquitous, such as Brooklyn's Red Hook neighbourhood, or Rwanda in Africa, or simply where community-led digital platforms are new forms of social infrastructure. Being co-designed and experimental, they open up possibilities for action and communication.

The malleable, shared environment of hyperlocal platforms has value because each is customised and dependent on the capacities of participants on the ground, rather than on external forces, to adapt them and direct their potentials. In smart urban-tech innovations, the focus is on speed, efficiency and control, but there is a huge need for democratic alternatives that represent 'a legitimate platform for the negotiation of complex factors', as architect Indy Johar, cofounder of Architecture 00, argues. As he points out, 'many of our civic-tech innovations seek to make direct democracy faster and more efficient – not necessarily smarter or wiser. They digitally enhance our reactive intelligence rather than the quality of representative democracy and our reflective and collective deep intelligences as a society.'[1]

In his article in this issue of △, 'Practices of the Minimum Viable Utopia' (pp 16–25), Adam Greenfield proposes that urban design must offload the 'dinosaurian' concept of the smart city that dominates its discourse and fetishises data, in favour of approaches that leverage technology but are not driven by it, where production is based on participation, 'democratising the ability to make useful things'. The layers of an interactive map built from time-based satellite imagery, for example, are not embedded with neutral data, but need critical analysis. This is exemplified in the work of Laura Kurgan and the Center for Spatial Research at Columbia University (pp 72–7) in the tragic context of Aleppo in Syria, which aims to reframe the narratives of the violence of war and its effects on cities and their communities.

Cities are interfaces open to interaction, and are therefore also hackable, or open to appropriation, write Martijn de Waal, Michiel de Lange and Matthijs Bouw in their analysis of collaborative citymaking (pp 50–57). They suggest that hackers alone should not contribute to systemic change, and that institutions such as local municipalities embedded within society must create policies that support public interests. Their Hackable City research reveals common strategies behind various hyperlocal models that frame and nurture new relationships and democratic practices.

All hyperlocal processes are defined by algorithms that, according to writer Paul Currion, are 'only a set of step-by-step instructions for carrying out a task'.[2] The work of coding needs to reflect the values necessary for open-source projects, which presents a challenge for design/management teams. In evaluating the increasing application of algorithms in humanitarian projects in combination with automation, Currion concludes that such a formula will fail to build an adequate transactional model for this field: 'Rather than be overtaken by software companies, we may need to become software companies – otherwise our lack of computer literacy means that the coding is going to be left to the hyperactive imagination of the hackathon.'[3]

Red Hook Initiative,
Red Hook WiFi,
Brooklyn,
New York,
2016

Red Hook WiFi provides free Internet access to local residents in an area with low broadband adoption rates, to close the digital divide. Its 'digital stewards', young adults aged between 19 and 24, promote the network's wider use by locals to support their lives, and the use of technology to promote community development more widely. Here three stewards check an outdoor router on the roof of the non-profit organisation.

As architect Usman Haque argues in 'VoiceOver: Citizen Empowerment Through Cultural Infrastructure' (pp 86–91), the rules behind the design of smart systems are all too often made behind closed doors, when it is citizens who need to be involved collectively in helping to shape society's algorithms. At their best, as his VoiceOver project in County Durham in the north of England demonstrates, hyperlocal networks and apps are collaboratively designed to enable peer communities to advance local interests by sharing human and physical resources.

Digital connectivity in rural villages extends a sense of community to a network beyond relatively isolated environments, maintains Katharine Willis in her article in this issue (pp 92–9), while in underprivileged urban centres many local programmes aim to close the digital divide and promote social connections through access to services and economic opportunities. When Hurricane Sandy struck the US in 2012, for example, severely limiting online access, the existing public Red Hook WiFi network for an isolated community in Brooklyn, New York, became a vital means of getting supplies and locating government aid workers. A mesh network still operating today, it uses decentralised technology, so that its nodes of routers sited on roofs as well as inside buildings can function when not connected to the Internet. A network with social incentives including a mapping platform, Red Hook WiFi relies on 'digital stewards', local young people who foster its functionality and maintain it with wholly open-source resources and software.

The Rise of the Geolocal
In the last few years the grassroots amenity of the hyperlocal has become strongly reflected in the information-sharing role of smartphones and social media in street protests such as the Arab Spring (triggered in Tunisia in 2010) and the global Occupy movement (from 2009 onwards), and by refugees sharing directions as they attempt to cross countries. An unprecedented number of people now make use of the high degree of precision about physical location that smartphones offer. In developing nations, usage of the device skyrocketed from 21 per cent of the population in 2013 to 37 per cent in 2015. In China in 2015 this was 52 per cent; and in the US 72 per cent.[4] An enormous amount of content available via the Internet can now be accessed and consumed from our phones.

While social media has been more recently buoyed by the development of the sharing economy and ecommerce, and the rise in blogs, it was in the late 1990s that websites first fostered multimedia, followed by rapid evolution in mobile content and applications around 2000. Digital platforms now have the capacity for their hyperlocal content to be created, distributed and managed in a more automated way, enabling a range of new perceptions and engagements. The growing extent of possibilities and motivation to manifest new functionalities is such that there is a greater focus on the distribution and sharing of information about daily life than on its quality.

The hyperlocal brings unknown aspects and layers of environmental features and characteristics into view, but who owns the unprecedented amount of data being mined daily by individuals and groups, hobbyists and professionals? The increasing popularity of 'checking in' to locations through

Hyperlocal networks and apps are collaboratively designed to enable peer communities to advance local interests by sharing human and physical resources.

Macro

Rwanda's population = 11.78 million.
Covering 5.2 million people

44% of the country's population with 3
buildings by 2019

Droneports

District Hospitals ●

50 Kilometre Range ———

100 Kilometre Range ———

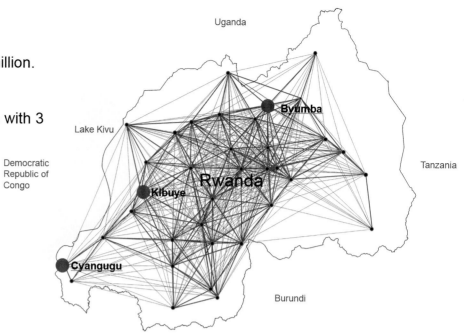

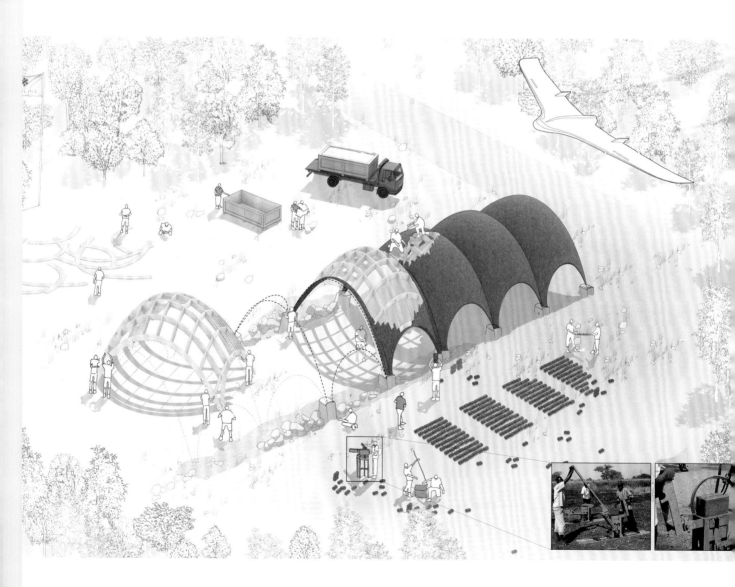

Foster + Partners,
Droneport,
Rwanda,
Africa,
2015–

The proposed network of
drone routes connects three
droneport locations with
district hospitals. It would
enable urgent and precious
supplies, particularly blood, to
be delivered to remote areas
on a massive scale, giving
support to 5.2 million people,
44 per cent of Rwanda's
population of 11.78 million. The
existing skeletal road network
covers just a fraction of the
country, while only a third of
Africans in rural areas live
within 2 kilometres (1.2 miles)
of an all-season road.

The construction sequence of
the new Droneport building
typology, an emblematic
vaulted brick structure.
Imagined as a kit-of-parts for
which only the basic formwork
and brick press machinery
are delivered to site, the
Droneport's raw materials –
clay and boulders – are locally
sourced.

geolocal media apps such as Foursquare (launched in 2009) and Pilgrim (2014–), as explored in this issue by José Luis de Vicente (pp 118–25), creates a rich, expanding pool of users' hyperlocal data. The rise of geolocal media has thus transformed the notion of the digital as a parallel dimension of physical reality into one that guides and informs people's knowledge of places through shared annotations.

Platforms and Toolsets for Navigating Complexity

Geolocal capacities are an immense resource for architects and urban planners to encode participatory parameters into their designs. As architects Will Gowland and Samantha Lee of UniversalAssemblyUnit argue in '△ 4D Hyperlocal Would Like to Use Your Current Location' (pp 104–9), the hyperlocal needs to develop its narratives through a bottom-up approach to GPS and real-time locating systems. Their visualisation apps provoke an alternative relationship to place, communication and social interaction to better suit user needs. The playful interactive 'Sentiment Architectures' systems and tools designed by Moritz Behrens (pp 98–103) develop the behavioural qualities of the urban mediascape, and boost public discourse by enabling citizens to directly express their feelings and views about civic concerns. Building multilayered visual representations of the city from social media imagery, for example Instagram posts, reveals their uneven distributions, as illustrated in the work of Lev Manovich and Agustin Indaco (pp 110–17), and is an incisive way for architects and planners to analyse urban environments to see how they change over time.

Multidisciplinary teams can change the stakes of a whole community by creating a culture of self-organisation, to share data, regenerate vacant spaces, implement local systems of upcycling and resources, and to crowdfund. Local platforms have recently been co-created by groups of resident activists, architectural and urban designers and planners such as Ecosistema Urbano and Saskia Beer. The ZO!City project, which Beer discusses in her article on pages 58–63, led to the founding of the TransformCity® online urban transformation platform for the district of Amstel3 in Amsterdam, supported by a distributed network structure. It is a digital tool that catalyses a sense of ownership for community members. While TransformCity enlightens other groups, Beer maintains that each platform must be made context-specific through local customisation.

The leveraging of environmental data by designers to empower citizens in their grasp of their built environments is possible by engaging the communicative and co-creative potential of such information. Until now, top-down simulation procedures of 3D urban observatories have produced results that are sometimes even difficult for architects and planners to understand. However, through the new generation of interactive hybrid-reality projective urban lab platforms that architect Bess Krietemeyer and colleagues at the Syracuse Center of Excellence in New York are developing as public exhibits (pp 36–43), a wide range of users can experience and analyse bioclimatic ambient energy flows and impacts. More intuitive perspectives of data and unconventional modes of visualisation elicit visitors' responses that become part of a library of open-source data.

Augmented Urbanism and Regional Infrastructures

Architects identify with hyperlocal processes because they introduce flexibility into design and transcend limitations in connectivity and programme through concrete demonstration of new alternatives. The geolocal, or locative media, bring versatility to architectural investigations of a fragmented, neglected area of the city like Segrate in Milan, writes Raffaele Pe (pp 78–85). They make places easier to navigate, and build perceptive capacities into the flow of information, freely creating knowledge and uniting a historical and geographical sense of belonging.

In contexts without adequate road and rail infrastructure such as rural Africa, the advantage offered by drones, or unmanned aerial vehicle (UAV) technology, is based on a bespoke connectivity and responsiveness to the needs of civil society. In 2011, a team of designers, engineers, computer programmers and entrepreneurs at the Singularity University, a public benefit corporation, developed networks of cheap cargo drones capable of transcending geographic barriers for humanitarian uses to carry urgent packages between base stations. These have since evolved as free prototypes by ARIA, a firm producing open-source autonomous logistics infrastructure, which was cofounded by one of the original team members, designer Arturo Pelayo. Foster + Partners, design for a Droneport in Rwanda, for example, introduces a new building typology that will be used for the transfer, via unmanned flying vehicles, of blood and other medical supplies to treat people with preventable diseases in remote areas. The intention is to create an entire drone network of Droneports, each including a health clinic, digital fabrication shop, postal room – an ecommerce trading hub and workshop where local people can manufacture drones.

UAV/drone technology is used not just to film and photograph urban sites, but to create 3D site models and map their different material ecologies, as the work of New York-based aerial video production company Marvel Vision demonstrates. UAVs enable digital mapping, largely due to programmability and range, and their GPS capabilities mean the maps are also geospatially accurate. They can therefore be programmed to survey a plot of land and create a digital 3D model, using photogrammetry combining photos and providing information such as distances between points, elevations of terrain and volumes of earth and structures. A young industry, UAVs have already significantly disrupted agriculture, development and energy, according to Pablo Marvel, CEO and cofounder of Marvel Vision: 'The true success and innovation will come from understanding this new aerial platform, and applying other softwares and technologies to find entirely new solutions.'[5]

Distributed Technologies

Hyperlocalism – thanks to collective intelligence enabled through open-source design – departs from traditional deterministic, purely scientific approaches. It enables planning and urban analysis to become relational and able to bridge the gap between resources that are tangible and measurable, and those that are not, through adaptive frameworks that demonstrate how multiple aspects of reality can be interacted with. Technologies are now an integral part of urban commons, and as such highly politically relevant to their identities as places with widely spread resources. This is maintained by Alejandro Zaera-Polo in his article 'The Posthuman City: Imminent Urban Commons' (pp 26–35), whose algorithmically responsive design processes incorporate climatic, environmental, programmatic and financial performances. Digital scanning and tracking and real-time feedback from these can create an adaptive substratum of open networks and improve the resilience of biodigital material systems, capacities Claudio Pasquero and Marco Poletto of ecoLogicStudio apply in their Solana Open Aviary project at a man-made nature reserve in Montenegro (see pp 44–9).

WXY architecture + urban design used Tygron Engine 3D modelling for their Gowanus Canal–Newtown Creek surge barrier project to obtain live intelligence on the impacts of different flood-protection scenarios. The study combines 3D visualisation and real-time feedback to support stakeholder discussions and negotiations on planning questions and possible outcomes. Similar to a gaming engine, the platform integrates GIS data layers, and not only allows stakeholders to test the implementation of alternative flood protection systems, but also to visualise how each intervention relates to its physical context, and the tradeoffs associated with each option. The Engine synthesises flood-map data, flood-protection intervention location data, and land-use data to inform users of how many residents and jobs are protected by a given scheme.

Locality and the Interdependency of Things

The Pokémon Go game, the first popular example of augmented reality using GPS location mapping, transforms the way players experience their local environments together. As one reviewer observed: 'For 21 million of you [reported numbers who bought the game on its release in July 2016], a game layer over a map of your city just became more useable than the map itself.'[6]

UAV/drone technology is used not just to film and photograph urban sites, but to create 3D site models and map their different material ecologies ...

Marvel Vision,
Antique aqueducts of
the Piedras River,
San Juan,
Puerto Rico,
2016

An orthomosaic, a collage of
hundreds of bird's-eye-view
photos taken from a drone
(UAV), which also enables digital
mapping. Innovation in the
use of drone footage of urban
sites is increasingly supporting
masterplanning, but also
enables 3D site models to be
constructed in a new way.

Marvel Vision,
Hull House,
Warwick,
New York,
2016

A maximum-precision 3D site
model of Hull House, created
as part of Marvel Vision's urban
planning research by stitching
GPS-embedded photos together
to give accurate X, Y and Z
placement.

WXY architecture +
urban design,
Newtown Creek Storm
Surge Barrier Study,
New York,
2015

above: Using Tygron Engine and Dynamic 3D models for a resiliency study commissioned by the NYC Economic Development Corporation, the architects modelled the costs and benefits of different storm surge barriers. They used a two-colour overlay producing a visualisation to indicate where the surge barrier system reduces flood risk in the project area.

below: Visualisation of property-ownership characteristics in the area of the project at Newtown Creek drawing on local land-use data.

Locality today is where the most stimulating design possibilities for doing things differently lie.

block_hood

Jose Sanchez/
Plethora Project,
Block'hood,
2016

Screenshot of Plethora's
neighbourhood-building
video game, in which more
than 80 building blocks can
be combined with complex
resource inputs and outputs
to encourage players to
think ecologically. The
game simulation includes
building blocks that use
real-world data. Crowd
simulation provides players
with environmental data
feedback on the habitats
being created.

While SimCity (invented by Will Wright in 1989) and WatchDogs (2013) encouraged players to appropriate a city's resources, architect Jose Sanchez, the inventor of the award-winning Block'hood neighbourhood building simulator video game (2016), maps information to real conditions, with participants encouraged to think about the interdependency of urban ecologies, and how they decay over time. Block'hood's different modes of use include: researching ecological solutions; playing with real-world environmental data; 'challenge', with limited resources; and 'modding', to alter and repurpose for any creative use.

Locality today is where the most stimulating design possibilities for doing things differently lie. Community empowerment and collaborative hyperlocal strategies are not absolute, but specific, helping to overcome scarcity of means and inequalities in flows of information and resources. As researcher John Bingham-Hall underlines in 'Imagined Community and Networked Hyperlocal Publics' (pp 64–71), we also need to consider the hyperlocal as a way to imagine the meaningfulness of place as a shared concern, as well as the benefit of hindsight in terms of what predigital communication practices have to offer.

The hyperlocal, then, is much more than a pliable digital layer of the city. As a participative civic ecology it supports social processes, networks and shared resources as part of community development. For urban design, which has long relied on static, linear and abstracting practices, to its detriment, the hyperlocal can enable open cycles of feedback loops that can be deployed much more effectively, increasing the social relevance of planning frameworks and pilot projects. For architects and designers collaborating with both specialist and community actors, the hyperlocal builds a fully engaged awareness of local life. The only way to influence an ecology in ways that matter is to be fully part of it. ⌂

Notes
1. Indy Johar in conversation with the author, June 2016. See also 00:/, *Compendium for the Civic Economy: What our Cities, Towns and Neighbourhoods Should Learn from 25 Trailblazers*, trancityxvaliz, 2011.
2. Paul Currion, 'Slave to the Algorithm', *Irin*, 11 July 2016: www.irinnews.org/opinion/2016/07/11/slave-algorithm.
3. *Ibid*.
4. Source: Jacob Poushter, 'Smartphone Ownership and Internet Usage Continues to Climb in Emerging Economies', Pew Research Center, 22 February 2016: www.pewglobal.org/2016/02/22/smartphone-ownership-and-internet-usage-continues-to-climb-in-emerging-economies/.
5. Pablo Marvel, interview with the author, 10 July 2016.
6. Alissa Walker, 'How Pokémon Go is Improving Your City', *Curbed*, 15 July 2016: www.curbed.com/2016/7/15/12189158/pokemon-go-improving-cities.

PRACTICES MINIMUM UTOPIA

Are smart cities really what we need? Or does their very nature go against the qualities of tolerance, resilience and face-to-face cooperation that are crucial to harmonious urban living? London-based writer and urbanist **Adam Greenfield** argues that networked technology would be put to far better use in citizen-led initiatives than in data-collection programmes dictated by a narrow elite.

OF THE VIABLE

15M protest banners,
Madrid,
22 March 2014

Banners decrying water privatisation at a peaceful protest by thousands of citizens against welfare cuts and the economic crisis, one of many by the 15M anti-austerity citizen movement (Indignados), which began life in the city's Puerta del Sol in 2011.

In the jargon of the 'lean development' methodology currently regnant in the discipline of software engineering, a 'minimum viable product' is one that has been released into the wild at the earliest possible moment, so that it can garner feedback on its design and performance directly from real users. This contrasts vividly with the traditional corporate approach to software development, which is to weigh applications down with an exhaustive catalogue of features and functions that are generally suggested by market research.

As the term suggests, a minimum viable product is shipped in an all but skeletal form, sporting just enough structure to work in service of an identifiable need. In principle, the intent is not necessarily to attract the largest possible audience, but rather to secure one that will constitute a reliable customer base for further elaborations of the product. From this point forward, that audience will play a crucial role in letting the developer know what features to incorporate next; over time, the product becomes a kind of iterative, collaborative co-creation.

There are certainly drawbacks to doing things this way. Lean development is strongly resonant with the contemporary Bay Area tech culture, with its cult of the 'founder', its callow and more-than-occasionally irresponsible emphasis on 'disruption' and its furniture of Soylent-fuelled 'brogrammers' crushing it in daily scrums. It undoubtedly shares with that culture an overly acute attention to the perceived prerogatives and interests of venture capitalists.

But there is nevertheless a certain appeal to it. Done well, the lean ethic of rapid iteration results in an arc of continuous incremental improvement. Developers avoid wasting time and resources building out functionality their customers neither want nor are willing to pay for, while the user base gets to participate in the crafting of a value proposition sensitively attuned to their actual needs and desires.

Could it be that it has something to teach the discipline of urban design? A single conception of how advanced information technology is to be deployed in the city utterly dominates urbanist discourse at present: the so-called 'smart city'. Curiously enough, it has a great deal in common with traditional processes of software development. It is maximalist, dinosaurian, intellectually lazy. Its emphases are driven by the capabilities and perspectives of multinational IT vendors, rather than the actual expressed needs of any identifiable urban community. Above all it is generic, offering only a placeless, one-size-fits-all template as abstract as any Microsoft or IBM ever devised for their customers.

With tongue only partway in cheek, then, might there not be room for a lean development approach to highly technologised urban environments? Rather than the single, top-down strategy espoused by the corporate architects of the smart city, this would be an experimental, participatory, iterative and, above all, multiple approach to the making of urban place – one that sensitively leverages advanced technology, but is not driven by it.

This presents us with an entirely different conception of the role data and data-driven tools might play in and for the city. As a way of thinking about the relationship between those tools and the development of a distinctively urban subjectivity, it is not merely subversive for the sake of being so, but offers a genuinely fruitful alternative to the intellectually bankrupt vision of the smart city. Its articulation hinges on four distinct components or movements: people making data, people making things, people making places, and people making networks.

PEOPLE MAKING DATA

One of the core premises of the smart city is that resource allocations and other policy decisions can be made on the basis of evidence sieved directly from urban flows by a vast, distributed sensing apparatus reaching into every sphere of life. Visions of this sort invariably fetishise data, placing it on a pedestal as something objective, transhistorical and, above all, nonpolitical – the endpoint of a process of argument, rather than its beginning. As patterns emerge from large, unstructured datasets, 'the data says' that fire stations should be placed here and not there, that these are the young citizens most likely to commit future crimes, that closing this route and opening that one will enhance the flow of city-centre traffic.

But this mentality neglects all the ways in which the decisions made in the process of gathering data are as salient to outcomes as the decisions made as a result of its collection. The approach being advocated here inverts this logic, by attending closely to matters of provenance. Just as a minimum viable product is designed to elicit actionable design information that will be used to refine future development, in an iterative process, so the urban probes imagined here are designed to turn up information about need, desire and fitness for purpose – transparently

DETROITography (Josh Akers,
Alex B Hill and Aaron Petcoff),
Property Praxis,
Detroit,
2015–

This collaborative mapping project by members
of DETROITography traces property ownership to
demonstrate how nearly 20 per cent of property
in the city is controlled by speculators, with the
majority of these structures vacant and collapsing.

nd in a way that is useful to all those who participate.

Such practices conceive of city people as the subjects of data production, rather than its passive objects, and therefore will tend to promote the broader emergence of critical data literacy. We will make 'better' collective decisions only when we routinely ask how a given dataset was made, why that collection was of interest in the first place, what alternatives might have been foreclosed in its acquisition, and most importantly of all, what the act of production makes of the people who participated in it? What we need to imagine is a decision framework in which it is natural to ask all these questions.

PEOPLE MAKING THINGS

Decision-making processes are not, of course, the only realm of human affairs currently being transformed by real-time access to networked data. The way we undertake material production, too, is yielding to the application of databased techniques, radically democratising the ability to make useful things.

In recent times a great deal has been made of the revolutionary potential of digital fabrication, and in fact an entire literature now exists suggesting that such techniques are inherently capable of undermining capitalism itself. For better or worse, a richer acquaintance with these tools and methods suggests

that this is not so, certainly not in anything like the near term. But when underwritten by freely downloadable specifications for a wide variety of useful tools and other objects, digital fabrication can indeed afford us a significant amount of local control over the structure and disposition of matter.

When fabricators are deployed at the neighbourhood scale, in clean storefront workshops under democratic community control, we enter a world of things produced for their use value rather than their exchange value, things that are designed in response to local need rather than desires churned by the spectacular economy. Equipped with open-source construction frameworks like WikiHouse and Grid Beam, we can even prototype, test and build useful structures, of sustainably produced materials and at relatively low cost.

Not nearly everyone will want to live in this way; not everyone will have the time or energy or wherewithal to do so, however much they might want to. But in order to credibly posit such practices as a fulcrum of large-scale change, it is not necessary to insist that all of us undertake them, all of the time – simply to provide for a situation in which more of us have the means and opportunity to do so than has broadly been the case in the developed world over the past half century.

DETROITography, Data,
Mapping, and Research
Justice workshop,
Cass Corridor/Midtown,
Detroit,
2015

Mapping a contested Detroit neighbourhood.
Members of a community-mapping workshop
conducted rapid interviews with people on the
street about the identity of the area to build a
narrative of place.

MIDCASS
TOWNCORR
IDOR

■ CASS CORRIDOR
■ OVERLAP
■ MIDTOWN

Data points based on interviews conducted
on 08/17/2015 as part of Data, Mapping, &
Research Justice workshop at Allied Media Projects.

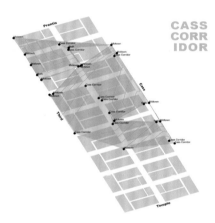

CASS
CORR
IDOR

MID
TOWN

PEOPLE MAKING PLACES

Digital fabrication techniques may suffice to create
prototype environments well suited to the requirements
of families and small groups. But generations of urban
theorists, from Lewis Mumford to Jane Jacobs to Doreen
Massey, have suggested that the place where cities truly
get 'remade' is in the public rather than the private sphere.
Here we imagine the collaborative use of open municipal
data to transform the environment at a larger scale.

This prospect hinges on the use of freely available,
open municipal datasets to identify vacant lots in the city
– whether these are publicly owned, or privately held by
speculators and 'warehoused' over the long term – and
reclaim them for citizen use. This is necessarily an ongoing
process of encounter, contestation and negotiation, but
it cannot get underway at scale before derelict parcels of
land are identified, as the Property Praxis mapping project
(illustrating the impact of speculation) does for Detroit, or
the 596 Acres initiative (by promoting local community
land access through tools and campaigns) does in
Brooklyn. Sometimes, indeed, a reclamation is undertaken
by citizen-activists directly aware of an abandoned site
because they walk by it every day, as at Madrid's Campo
de Cebada, an abandoned commercial development site
turned social centre.

Zuloark,
El Campo de Cebada,
Madrid,
2013

Open-air concerts every Sunday are a feature
of El Campo de Cebada in the La Latina
neighbourhood of Madrid created in 2012
by architects Zuloark with local residents.

uloark,
l Campo de Cebada,
adrid,
012

'The Barley Field' (Cebada), an experimental public facility created as
a non-authorship project by architects Zuloark with residents in the
working-class La Latina district of Madrid in 2010. With street furniture,
mobile planters and inflatable swimming pools, it is used for their
weekly meetings and for music, film and performance events, open-air
celebrations, skating and tai chi.

t New York Farms organic vegetable
den, Brooklyn, New York

t: One of the organic vegetable gardens for the local
munity managed by East New York Farms, which
been promoting local sustainable agriculture and
munity-led economic development in the district
e 1998.

Nomadic Green, Prinzessinengarten, Kreuzberg,
Berlin,
2012

Biological, social and cultural diversity is fostered at Prinzessinengarten's community plots
for organic vegetable growing, a project that began life in 2009 on a pilot basis on a site in
Moritzplatz that had been wasteland for more than 50 years.

below: Debating continues into the early hours at Nuit Debout gatherings, with some protestors sleeping in tents and makeshift shelters in the camp occupying the square.

below middle: Nuit Debout –'rise up at night' – has seen nocturnal protest gatherings of more than a thousand people of all ages at Place de la République, Paris (pictured), and in other cities such as Toulouse, Lyons, Nantes, and Brussels in Belgium, debating issues such as housing, refugees, national security and labour rights.

This tactic is best suited to postindustrial cities beset by crises of depopulation, or perhaps ones where a previous housing bubble has burst, where in either case the retreat of investment has transformed entire swathes of the city into desolate sacrifice zones. Even in urban environments not subject to these conditions, though, it is occasionally possible for neighbours to fashion public space directly; for example, the historically Puerto Rican community gardens of New York's Lower East Side, Berlin's Prinzessinnengarten, the undercroft of London's Southbank Centre, or projects like the curious Institute for (X) in Aarhus, Denmark, where parts of an abandoned railway freight yard were recovered for community use. Liberated in this way, these lots and parcels can become sites for experiments in land use that are driven by prerogatives other than those of commercial real-estate speculation, ends as various as silent contemplation, the provision of food security or the establishment of an etymologically literal 'thing' – a place for the practice of democracy.

LIBERATED IN THIS WAY, THESE LOTS AND PARCELS CAN BECOME SITES FOR EXPERIMENTS IN LAND USE THAT ARE DRIVEN BY PREROGATIVES OTHER THAN THOSE OF COMMERCIAL REAL-ESTATE SPECULATION

below top: The streets of the Central Business District were occupied in an orderly way by tens of thousands of Hong Kong residents demanding true universal suffrage, many of them sheltering in tents and creating on-site protest art.

below bottom: The yellow umbrella widely used at the Umbrella Revolution protests in Hong Kong's Central Business District became a symbol of a generation fighting for democracy, used to protect protestors from tear gas, pepper spray and rain, and to carry painted political slogans.

PEOPLE MAKING NETWORKS

Democracy, of course, is a process, not an event. It is not something that happens in a voting booth every four or five years, but a state of being that must be continuously reproduced through the investment of active effort. As the Spanish 15M and the global Occupy movement reminded us in 2011 – as Hong Kong's 2014 Umbrella uprising and the 2016 Nuit Debout demonstrations in France have, in years since – the popular assembly retains considerable potency as a mode of self-governance. But among the many and well-known drawbacks it suffers from, perhaps the one that most decisively cripples its broader applicability is the problem of availability.

This is not so much, as might be thought, an explicit problem of scale; Occupy developed innovative 'people's microphone' and hand-signalling techniques to coordinate decision-making processes among large groups, and in any event it is likely that for most ordinary purposes communities will tend to gather in effective cells of around the Dunbar size of 150. But sincere participation imposes burdens; given the necessity of showing up to work, the claims on our time posed by our obligations to others and the simple reality of exhaustion, it is not always realistic, or fair, to expect every member of a community to invest the effort and energy required by the face-to-face practice of decision by assembly.

This is why we need to call upon networked architectures of participation like the brilliant Loomio, a mobile application that allows its users to propose courses of action, discuss their merits and drawbacks, and vote on their adoption. By no coincidence, Loomio was developed by veterans of the Occupy movement, and its design was directly informed by their experience.

This is not the same thing as, let alone a replacement for, a face-to-face assembly, but it does allow people to engage asynchronously, as they find the time and energy. It also allows local experimental sites and projects to be linked as nodes in a broader mesh of participatory, community-based action.

We need to be clear that there is no magic about networks. 'Decentralised' and 'distributed' are ultimately ways of describing topographies of connection, not values in themselves. Organising something as a network does not do the necessary work of articulating what kind of world one wants to call into being, except

A MINIMUM VIABLE APPROACH TO THE MAKING OF PLACE CHARGES US TO IMAGINE WAYS WE MIGHT USE NETWORKED TECHNOLOGY TO MAKE URBAN FORM(S) AND EXPERIENCE(S) THAT RESPOND TO OUR OWN NEEDS AND DESIRES, AND NOT THOSE OF THE MULTINATIONAL TECHNOLOGY VENDORS, THEIR THOUGHTLESS ENABLERS IN THE MEDIA, OR THE FINANCIAL AND POLITICAL ELITES WE SO OFTEN FIND THEM ENMESHED WITH.

erhaps along a single organisational axis. But it does allow people to work locally, while remaining coordinated with and learning from other communities that are dealing with similar issues, whether those communities are across town or on the other side of the world. Such a scheme lets local particularity flourish, without fetishising 'the local' for its own sake.

OVARDS THE MINIMUM VIABLE UTOPIA

ndependent of whatever specific local innovations people are able to develop, it is clear that the lean methodology described here is likely to improve on the top-down smart city, along several axes of consideration.

Consider that the smart city offers a conception of urban citizenship delivered and received like any other consumer product. It constructs an urban subject active only to the extent that he or she shoulders responsibilities the public sector has withdrawn from, and is otherwise fundamentally passive. The primary role imagined for such subjects is the generation of data for analysis and the construction of projective models.

Each of the tactics described here is different. Each asks of us that we actively work to fashion our environment, in collaboration with our neighbours and potentially in contestation of other uses. These are concrete circumstances that, through 'developing and exercising one's capacities [and] participating in determining one's action and the conditions of one's action', fulfill the preconditions of justice articulated by American social theorist Iris Marion Young.[1]

A city built up in this way, though, would also simply be a vastly more pleasant place to live in than one decreed from the top down. My fundamental concern is not so much that living in a smart city would be a dystopian nightmare. It is frankly that the residents of any city that had been rendered 'smart' in the way contemporary discourse suggests would themselves be nightmares to encounter and deal with: touchy, needy, self-absorbed, and broadly incapable of negotiating the shared use of environments and resources.

What kinds of subjects and subjectivities tend to be reproduced by smart-city technologies? I think we have a pretty clear sense of the answer. Consider that 'optimised' urban management tends to create epistemic and experiential bubbles, acting to prospectively eliminate the daily frictions that force us to confront the other, and acknowledge the validity of that other's claims to the city.

For example, I once saw a data-analytics company give a presentation where both the headline on their PowerPoint deck and the value proposition they were claiming for their product was literally and in so many words 'Find People Like Me'. But that is not how cities work. That is not, even remotely, what cities are for. Cities are, by definition, sites for the practice of cosmopolitanism; anyone who chooses to live in one had better expect that along with the enhanced economic opportunity comes the unavoidable necessity of negotiating with people who are different, who hold values and prerogatives that diverge from one's own. It is that constant exposure to difference that generates the worldly, tolerant, resilient, feisty personality we associate with big cities around the world and throughout human history.

A minimum viable approach to the making of place charges us to imagine ways we might use networked technology to make urban form(s) and experience(s) that respond to our own needs and desires, and not those of the multinational technology vendors, their thoughtless enablers in the media, or the financial and political elites we so often find them enmeshed with. In doing so, we rediscover techniques of self-provision and self-governance that hinge on face-to-face collaboration, that restore to us some sense of control over the circumstances of our lives, that develop in us that organic competence for the urban that we have recognised as the birthright of big-city people since human beings first started gathering in cities.

Undergirded by technology that we already have in hand, built on practices of social organisation we have relied upon since the dawn of recorded history, this modest kind of utopia, at least, is well within reach. It is now up to us as to whether or not we will ever get to live there. ∆

Note
1. Iris Marion Young, *Justice and the Politics of Difference*, Princeton University Press (Princeton, NJ), 1990, p 37.

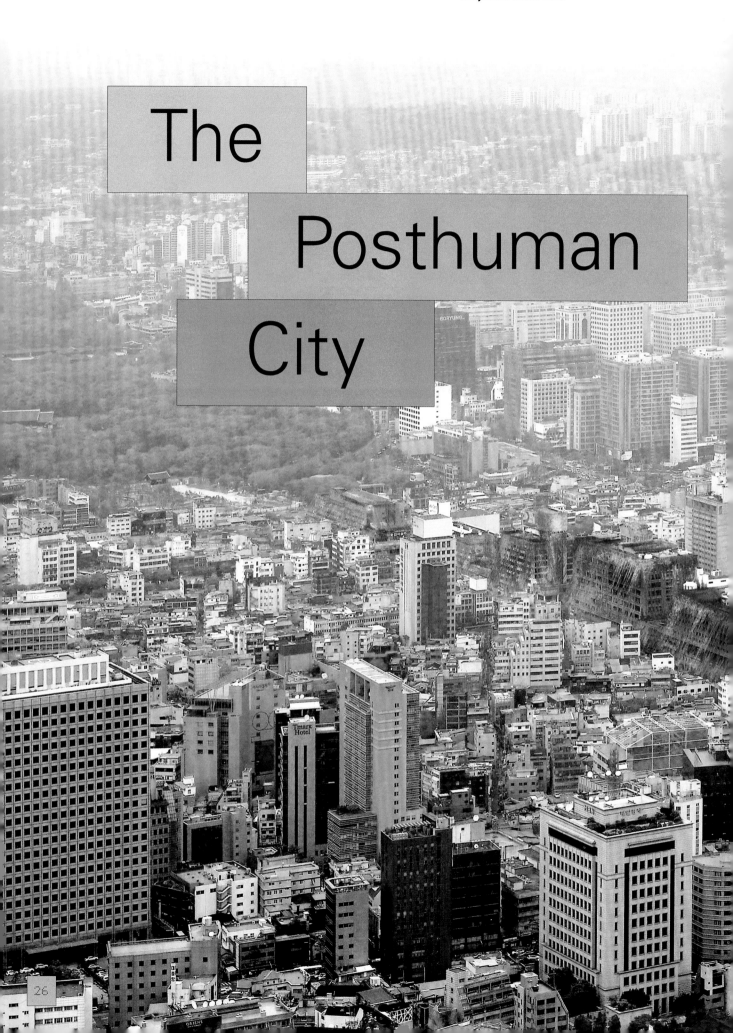

Alejandro Zaera-Polo

The Posthuman City

Aerial view of Seun Sangga, formerly the Kim Swoo Geun megastructure built in the late 1960s with seven connected shopping centres, the first downtown redevelopment project in South Korea. The proposal uses the building as a topography, with a new vegetation and artificial sierra linking Bugak-San and Nam-San, the north and south hills of traditional Seoul.

Imminent Urban Commons

Urban planning has long been governed by the classification of human activities – work, residence, leisure and transport. However, this approach is ill suited to addressing the ever more pressing environmental concerns of our age. **Alejandro Zaera-Polo** – Artistic Codirector of the Seoul Biennale of Architecture and Urbanism 2017 and cofounder with Maider Llaguno of architecture practice AZPML – argues for broad new urban cosmologies and an embracing of technology to enhance the democracy of urbanism.

Since the 18th century, when the Western world became human-centred, mankind has been constantly evolving. So too has the very concept of the human. In the Anthropocene, humans have become capable of modifying natural ecosystems, geological structures, even the climate. They have become so powerful that it is increasingly difficult to delimit the natural from the artificial. As the most populated human environment, cities are a central focus of these transformations, and are primarily designed around human functions. This, despite the fact that the crucial questions they need to address – air pollution, rising water levels, draught, heat island effect, deforestation, biodiversity, food security, automatised work, inequality – are primarily driven by non-human – some would say posthuman – concerns.

In 1933, Le Corbusier and a few other members of the Congrès International d'Architecture Moderne (CIAM) discussed the principles which were to constitute the *Athens Charter*, a document aimed at orchestrating the technologies of the artificial into a proposal for the future of cities.[1] Forming the spine of this proposal was a classification of human activities around four urban functions: work, residence, leisure and transport. This functional classification has structured urban planning policies ever since, but its human-centred approach appears now to be unable to address the problems of posthuman civilisation.

Citizens are increasingly aware that they inhabit ecosystems transcending their specific urban realms, which are crucially mediated by technology. For cities to address the challenges of the Anthropocene, in which the primeval elements – air, water, energy and earth – have become artificial, humanised and politicised, they need to redefine themselves as a much broader entity: one that is concerned with machines, animals, plants and the collective of all their peer cities. Citizens will have to develop a cosmopolitical perspective of the world at large as their cosmologies will no longer be limited to the conceptualisation of the natural elements, but crucially mediated by the technologies that feed us, transport us, condition our environments, recycle our refuse, produce our clothes or connect us to each other.[2] Like air, water, energy and living creatures, technologies are an integral part of the imminent urban 'commons'. This cocktail of themes infuses the first Seoul Biennale of Architecture and Urbanism, to be staged from September 2017.

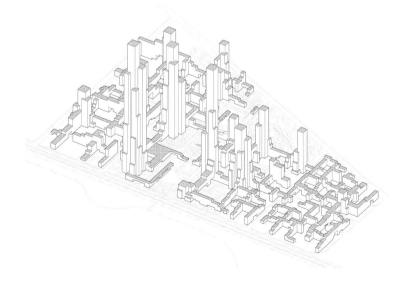

AZPML,
Eroded Urbanism,
Shenzhen Bay,
China,
2014

This view explains how the stepping of the urban fabric enables an effective structural performance of the tall buildings while providing opportunities for sky gardens and other high-level intense vegetation.

Posthuman Cosmologies

Ancient cosmologies were mechanisms of comprehension of the natural world which enabled cultures to understand and operate within the natural environment. The oldest ones predated human settlements and were aimed at explaining natural phenomena and regulating the modes of relation between humans and nature through a mythical interpretation of the cosmos. As the human environment became increasingly controlled by technology, and as politics – a word derived from the Greek *politika*, meaning 'affairs of cities' – came to replace cosmologies as systems of knowledge and governance, typology and monumentality became primary tools for urbanism, with the structure of human relations prevailing over the physical determinations of the environment.

An entirely new set of urban technologies – smartphones, GPS, electromobility, biotechnology – have since appeared, radically transforming urban protocols and experiences, while remaining largely outside the practices of urban planners and designers who are still trapped in the humanistic precepts of modern urbanism. The current prevalence of artificial environments – cities – and politics has naturalised technology and de-politicised nature. The pressing nature of ecological concerns and the scale of technological developments call for the imminent city to re-politicise both nature and technology and construct new urban cosmologies able to develop new urban sensibilities.

Far from producing urbanity, humanist urban functionalism has dismantled the commons and undermined urban democracy. Cities have become sources of extreme inequality and environmental degradation, which are even threatening their own subsistence, and are pointing at insurmountable contradictions at the core of the current modes of economic integration. Theorists like Jeremy Rifkin and Paul Mason argue that we are already entering a postcapitalist world in which politics are shifting from a focus on capital and labour, to a focus on energy and resources.[3] They have proposed new economies – shared economies of zero marginal costs – that would be driven by new technologies: peer-to-peer organisations, big data, sustainable energy sources and carbon-neutral technologies likely to become the drivers of a new kind of urban politics.

Cities have also become the largest human habitat, and therefore the epicentres of global warming, air pollution and a variety of ecological malaises. Naomi Klein has pointed at the fundamental opposition between capitalist growth and the limited natural resources of the earth, and questioned the capacity of capitalist regimes to resolve an imminent ecological catastrophe.[4] The decline of capitalism has loaded technology – and, more precisely, urban technologies – with an unprecedented political relevance. Cities have become a crucial intersection between technology and politics where the equations between wealth, labour, resources and energy have to be reset to address the current shortcomings of neo-liberal economies.

Does this scenario imply that the work of urbanists and architects has become futile, and that the new commons will be entirely developed within the virtual space of the Internet and realm of algorithms? Has urbanism been expelled from contemporary politics, now at the mercy of securitisation and capital redistribution? Some economists argue that urban planning, housing and real estate hold the key to resolving inequality.[5] For cities to become devices for the common good rather than instruments producing power structures (and therefore inequality or ecological destruction), imminent urban technologies need to locate resources and technologies at their core. Rather than splitting urban life into functions easily captured by power, these imminent urban commons need to become instruments of devolution and ecological awareness, constructed transversally across technologies and resources.

Cities have become sources of extreme inequality and environmental degradation, which are even threatening their own subsistence, and are pointing at insurmountable contradictions at the core of the current modes of economic integration.

Air

Air is the element that most intimately binds all humans on earth together. However, seven million people die every year from exposure to air-induced diseases.[6] Delhi, Cairo, Beijing, Mexico City and many other major cities are plagued by toxic air. New technologies being developed enable cities to increase air exchange rates and natural ventilation technologies, both at the scale of buildings and at a city-wide scale. Climate-altering technologies such as pollution mitigation, cloud seeding, carbon sequestration and adiabatic cooling are some of the instruments able to mitigate anthropogenic effects on climate and forge a contemporary cosmopolitics of air to bring about both new cultural constructs and design opportunities.

The hydrologic cycle of cities involves more than preventing damage from rising sea levels. Water retention for urban comfort, water collection and water treatment systems are also important areas of development.

Water

Global warming and climate change are not only distorting traditional climate patterns, but also reshaping the earth itself. Rising sea levels are expected to have a massive impact on cities around the world in the coming decades, and their impact is already felt through disasters and in plummeting real estate values. Urban waterfronts and riverfronts, traditionally key territories of urban life, are now threatened by rising water levels.

But water is also critical in other ways. The hydrologic cycle of cities involves more than preventing damage from rising sea levels. Water retention for urban comfort, water collection and water treatment systems are also important areas of development. By 2050 a third of the people on Earth may lack a clean, secure source of water.[7] Each component in the urban water cycle brings its own benefits and challenges. The systematic replacement of impermeable/non-osmotic pavements, such as asphalt surfaces covering a large percentage of urban land; the introduction of bioswales or the recovery of buried streams within cities; and the development of water-retaining materials for building envelopes – these are some of the current possibilities for urban practices likely to change the landscape of future cities.

AZPML,
Eroded Urbanism,
Shenzhen Bay,
China,
2014

Continuous roofscape, promenades and passageways. The bird's-eye view conveys a concern with the urban microclimate, with extensive vegetation of the dense urban fabric used as a means to neutralise the heat island effects triggered by high-density urbanisation.

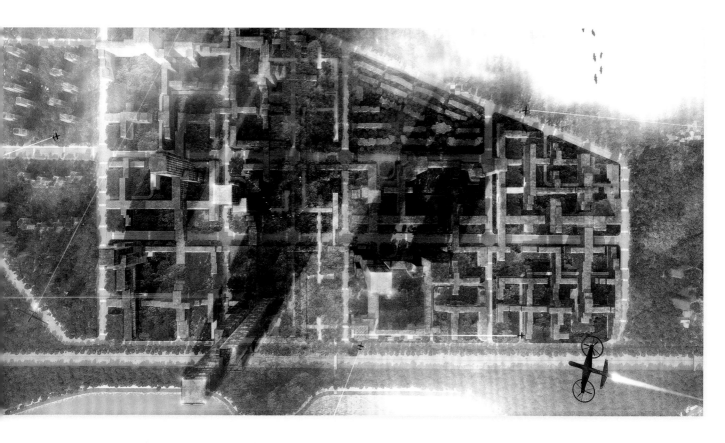

Fire

Fire – the placeholder for energy – is one of the vital questions that cities need to address in the very near future. Fossil fuel consumption is not only depleting natural resources, but, most importantly, releasing carbon into the atmosphere and producing climate change, which is in turn causing pollution health hazards and raising water levels. Buildings consume 40 per cent of global energy and 40 per cent of global resources, and produce 48 per cent of carbon emissions, with large energy use concentrated in urban centres.[8] The development of solar, wind, tidal and ground-sourced energy sources able to power cities without resorting to the combustion of fossil fuels will profoundly redefine the new urban cosmopolitics. Fossil fuel ecologies triggered massive geopolitical conflicts in the Middle East, Central America and Southern Russia, but the shift to sustainable sources will trigger politics articulating consumption patterns with sustainable energy source potentials. As sustainable energy is primarily mediated through electricity, it needs to be resolved with locally responsive strategies, as the potentials of sustainable energy sources vary depending on climate and geology. A new cosmopolitics of sustainable sources would do away with global geopolitics and national energy standards, and would take climatic variations into account.

Earth

Earth is a complex substance incorporating topography and *humus* – the bioactive layer of the soil. It could also be related to notions such as carbon footprint, which establish equivalences between land-measuring units and their capacity to produce energy from sustainable sources, or to absorb carbon and perform within hydrological cycles. Transferring surface energy budgets from geophysics and microclimatology to architecture can account for the relationship between land, hydrology, energy and airflow.[9] Biotechnologies – urban farming, hydroponics, and algae cultures with the ability to produce food, biofuels and even light cities – are some of the fastest-growing technologies with urban applications. Green building envelopes – roofs and walls – are capable of not only increasing a building's albedo (reflectivity coefficient),[10] but also retaining natural humidity in the urban microclimate, absorbing CO_2, producing oxygen, and reducing the heat island effect. These technologies have yet to be incorporated into buildings as an integral part of the earth's surface, an intrinsic component of the imminent urban cosmologies.

below: The image displays a series of tests of the algorithmic excavation of the primitive ideal urban fabric.

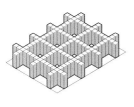 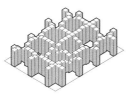 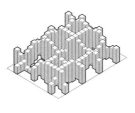 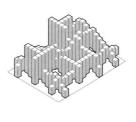 

0% erosion   25% erosion   47% erosion   60% erosion   75% erosion

Contours of Velocity Magnitude (m/s)

May 03, 2014
ANSYS Fluent 14.5 (3d, dp, pbns, ske)

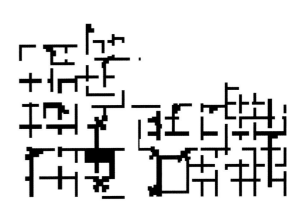

above: Computational fluid dynamics (CFD) simulation of wind flow. In order to improve the microclimatic conditions, an ideally designed square grid has been eroded specifically through an algorithm to produce an ideal balance between ventilation and wind comfort.

above: The fabric is formed by a solid grid of 15-metre-high (50-foot) buildings surrounding a series of adjacent plazas, in order to provide a multifunctional fabric suitable for either residential or commercial uses, and naturally ventilated.

Sensing

The proliferation of sensors in the environment is one of the most defining facts of the imminent urban milieu. A normal car alone may contain over one hundred sensors to control its functions. A common domestic thermostat measures temperature once per second with a precision of half a degree. When these sensors become interconnected, an unprecedented common, novel in sensibility, will create a collective, global sensorium. Some websites are already constructing this data-based sensorium on an open-source status. Personal environmental sensors in development, when connected to smartphones, will be able to distribute instant remote sensing to urban populations, enabling constant updates on the urban environment, transport, security, temperature, wind, humidity, pollution and many other factors. These will become crucial tools reacting to changing environmental urban patterns and generating an unprecedented consciousness about our urban environments. The time when local air quality becomes a collective obsession and starts driving real estate values is imminent.

Connecting

One of the more powerful imminent commons has been created by the emergence of social media on the Internet. These technologies have entirely reshaped the protocols of communication and relations between citizens. The possibility of connecting domestic control mechanisms with smartphones may also reshape the way in which we relate to our jobs or domestic infrastructures, and look likely to transform the structures of governance. Initiatives are testing possibilities to make governance a more democratic process by engaging citizens in instant decision making. Questions of control and privacy are currently some of the most pressing for governments, corporations and lawmakers – and surely for architects and urbanists. The development of unprecedented forms of domesticity, work and leisure, their deterritorialisation and impact in urban cultures and politics is also one of the most important of imminent urban realms' evolutionary patterns.

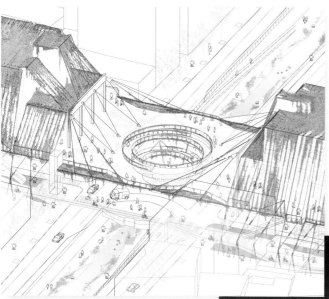

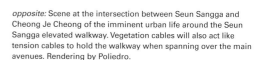

opposite: Scene at the intersection between Seun Sangga and Cheong Je Cheong of the imminent urban life around the Seun Sangga elevated walkway. Vegetation cables will also act like tension cables to hold the walkway when spanning over the main avenues. Rendering by Poliedro.

below: A scene of the imminent urban life along the future Seun Sangga elevated walkway, populated by individual electromobility and unipersonal vehicles. The existing 1960s megastructure will be entirely covered with steel cable meshes where creepers will grow. Rendering by Poliedro.

AZPML,
Seun Sangga arcade,
Seoul,
South Korea,
2015

above: The elevation of the proposed Seun Sangga project shows the structural cables that will support the elevated walkways and the growth of creepers, forming a deciduous vegetation veil in summer while allowing light through in winter.

Moving

Transportation is one of the most energy-intensive activities in contemporary cities, accounting for a large percentage of overall carbon emissions. Unipersonal electric vehicles and self-driven vehicles are likely to change urban traffic beyond recognition, and a number of global companies are addressing the development of these technologies. Electromobility and sharing schemes for unipersonal or logistic vehicles are now spreading worldwide, anticipating decentralised urban transport infrastructures with a minimal carbon footprint. Logistics are an important part of these developments dealing with energy consumption, carbon emissions and pollution. Amazon Robotics' warehouse systems and drone experiments are some of the new initiatives being tested to make transportation and shipping in cities more efficient.

Sharing

Some of the most transformative processes triggered by ubiquitous computing and Web-enabled devices relate to the possibility of sharing services and goods in time, including Airbnb, bicycle and car-share schemes, co-working spaces, and other urban processes based on shared economies. Today's city, inherited from modernist planning, is primarily regulated by private property laws, yet increasingly determined by shared ownership, where social media and ubiquitous mobile devices hold the key to the development of new urban protocols, institutions, typologies and experiences. The management of resources and energy though sharing, recycling or optimisation through the deployment of new technologies is increasing, and current legislation needs to shift towards the normalisation of sharing protocols. The potentials of the urbanisation of technology give rise to new potentials for architecture to engage with these crucial processes of contemporary urban culture.

Making

If the late capitalist city is characterised by the exile of production from the urban core, the takeover of financial services and the securitisation of the city through residential markets as a key component of urban economies, there are now new technologies of digital fabrication, laser 3D scanning, 3D printing and robotics relocating some high-value fabrication activities back to the urban cores. The impact of these technologies on urban economies signals the return of production to the city, and its constitution into an urban common of the emerging *homo faber* – humans that can control their environment through tools.

Shared spaces of production, rentable fabrication equipment, and processing recycled or reclaimed materials are key aspects of this shift in production. Inexpensive CNC routers and 3D printers, the rise of Etsy and Pinterest, open-source software and free tutorials have encouraged a wave of DIY production generating small-scale urban industry. A revision of new urban production technologies and how they may be reinserted in the urban fabric is now an important field of consideration and research.

Recycling

Metropolitan governments have been giving increasing attention to the collection, sorting and recycling of urban waste and biosolids. This has reached a geopolitical dimension, with regional and even transcontinental systems of treating refuse. The cultural dimension of recycling protocols is enormous and directly impacts on citizens and their perceptions of the identity of the city. Japan, for example, has been at the forefront of incubating a collective consciousness about recycling and installing infrastructure to optimise urban metabolism. Many cities have attempted to follow the Japanese example, only to realise the cultural obstacles of doing so. The physical structure of the city itself has been a subject of recycling activities, with an increasing rate of preservation and retrofitting of existing urban infrastructures. Waste management issues are intertwined with land management and pollution, as landfills and carbon dioxide emissions now influence the processing of waste. Tagging programmes for tracking the waste management process have been experimented with by researchers aiming to reveal the hidden systems that govern our unwanted possessions, and potentially to develop more intelligent systems for these processes.[11]

It appears inevitable for urban practices of the immediate future to incorporate these emerging technologies in fields where the new urban commons are to be found, ranging from governance to production. Especially because urban technologies based on human functions have now become mechanisms to divide and to control power rather than to produce resilient commonality, imminent cosmologies will need to address the politics of the posthuman commons – resources and technologies – in order to enable urbanistic practices that are both artificially mediated and collective.

left: Perspective of the administration building, an artificial mountain wrapped in louvre/planters, which protect the facade from solar exposure while growing hydroponic vegetation. This retains the natural humidity levels while also acting as a naturally adjustable sunshade. Rendering by SBDA.

Algorithmic, Eroded Urbanism

These concerns underpin many of the recent proposals by architecture practice AZPML, particularly those with an urban scope. 'Eroded Urbanism' (2014) was a masterplan design proposal for a hyper-dense urban district of the Chinese city of Shenzhen. Seun Sangga Artificial Sierra (2015) was a competition proposal for the redevelopment of the Seun Sangga megastructure in central Seoul and its reconversion into an artificial mountain chain linking the Bukhansan with the Namsan mountains, as a green corridor which would contribute to carbon trapping, oxygenation and pollination of the city centre. The Yantai Harbour Masterplan (2013) was a proposal for an expansion by 1 million inhabitants to Yantai City, Shandong, China, on the former grounds of the harbour. Designs for two large-scale buildings for Weifang University (2015), also in Shandong Province, and the redevelopment of a power station in Wedel, Germany (2013), were based on combinatorial formal strategies which foster the flexibility of the architecture, and the systematic deployment of vegetated envelopes to produce environmental improvements. The versatility of algorithmically driven design enables evolutionary masterplanning, as well as flexible land use and programmatic determinations. Building patterns and materials were set out and made responsive to climatic exposure considerations and air quality.

Both in Shenzhen and in Weifang, the buildings are part of a continuum of different microclimates, and form is constructed as accretions of cells with a contingent, 'voxelised' aesthetic. There is a deliberate exploration of the simplified aesthetics of Big Data, where increasing computing capacity enables tighter approximations to balance urban processes, at the expense of a reduction of formal specificity. The designs were optimised through an algorithmically responsive design process to incorporate climatic, environmental, programmatic and financial performances. Erosion and the systematic use of vegetation on the surfaces are some of the concrete tactics used in these projects.

Like in 1933, our current age is marked by vast technological development which needs to be incorporated far more into the ways we conceive and design cities within wider global ecologies. Just as the *Athens Charter* was able to synthesise human-centred politics around the division of functions, the arcane elements of air, water, fire and earth and the rise of artificially mediated collectivities and metabolic processes enabled by the emerging technologies of sensing, sharing, moving, making or recycling should become the central concern of a posthuman urbanism. An update of the modernist human-centred functions that still form the spine of urban practice is now imminent. ⌂

AZPML,
Weifang University,
Weifang City,
Shandong Province,
China,
2015

below: The new canteen displays the intensive green roof of this building, which will help the campus to retain natural humidity levels. The roof ramps are used both to move between levels and to create a natural auditorium towards the University's central quad. Rendering by SBDA.

Notes

1. Le Corbusier, Jean Giraudoux and Jeanne de Villeneuve, *La Charte d'Athènes*, Plon, Paris, 1943; English translation, *The Athens Charter* (trans Anthony Eardley), Grossman (New York), 1973.
2. See Albena Yaneva and Alejandro Zaera-Polo, *What is Cosmopolital Design? Design, Nature and the Built Environment*, Ashgate (Farnham), 2015.
3. Jeremy Rifkin, *The Zero Marginal Cost Society: The Internet of Things, the Collaborative Commons, and the Eclipse of Capitalism*, Macmillan (London), 2014; Paul Mason, *PostCapitalism: A Guide to Our Future*, Allen Lane (London), 2015; Paul Mason, 'The End of Capitalism Has Begun', *The Guardian*, 17 July 2015, http://www.theguardian.com/books/2015/jul/17/postcapitalism-end-of-capitalism-begun.
4. Naomi Klein, *This Changes Everything: Capitalism vs. the Climate*, Simon & Schuster (New York), 2014.
5. Matthew Rognlie, *Deciphering the Fall and Rise in the Net Capital Share*, BPEA Conference Draft, 19–20 March 2015, http://www.brookings.edu/~/media/projects/bpea/spring-2015/2015a_rognlie.pdf; Thomas Piketty, *Capital in the Twenty-First Century*, Harvard University Press (Cambridge, MA), 2014.
6. World Health Organization, news release, March 2014, http://www.who.int/mediacentre/news/releases/2014/air-pollution/en/.
7. 'A Freshwater Crisis': see *National Geographic*, April 2010: *Water: A Special Issue*.
8. 'Why Buildings', United Nations Environment Program, http://www.unep.org/sbci/AboutSBCI/Background.asp.
9. 'Surface Energy Budget', NASA Earth Observatory, http://earthobservatory.nasa.gov/Features/EnergyBalance/page5.php.
10. Albedo is the earth's reflectivity, another parameter derived from meteorology and energy budgets commonly applied to building envelopes: see *Environmental Encyclopedia*, 3rd edn, Thompson Gale (Detroit), 2003.
11. See Carlo Ratti and Sense*able* City Lab, *Trash|Track*, http://senseable.mit.edu/trashtrack/.

Bess Krietemeyer

Projective Empowerment

Co-creative Sustainable Design Processes

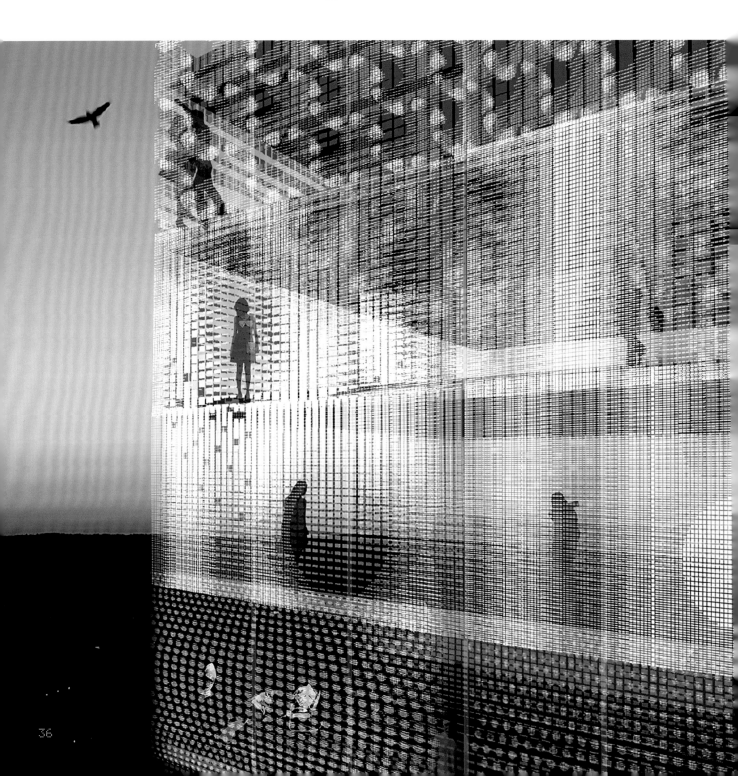

The human body's perception of ambient energy flows in the built environment is a complex yet important consideration in designing high-performance architectural systems, buildings and cities. **Bess Krietemeyer**, Assistant Professor at the School of Architecture at Syracuse University and Head of the Interactive Design and Visualization Lab (IDVL) at the Syracuse Center of Excellence, explores how interactive hybrid-reality platforms for experiencing and analysing bioclimatic flows in architectural design are empowering designers and end users to engage in collaborative design processes from diverse viewpoints and across spatial scales.

How can we leverage the availability of environmental data within public venues to simultaneously educate and empower citizens? Despite the increasing uses of environmentally data-rich, bottom-up networking within cities, design decision-making typically occurs as a top-down process. It is often based on a narrow and regulated scope of how the built environment impacts design and the people who live there, but not necessarily the other way around. There is enormous potential in integrating information such as user trends, preferences, movement patterns and energetic data into the design decision-making process, but this can be difficult to collect, parse and communicate in meaningful ways to the general public. Furthermore, existing simulation data is often accepted as objective and unchanging, overlooking the unpredictability of intuitive user decisions.

The intention of the research and design experimentation undertaken by a team of architects, engineers, computer scientists and artists at the Interactive Design and Visualization Lab (IDVL) at the Syracuse Center of Excellence (SyracuseCoE), in collaboration with visual artists and interactive software developers NOIRFLUX and the Milton J Rubenstein Museum of Science and Technology (MoST), is to explore the ways emerging visualisation technologies can be utilised to incorporate intuitive user input into projective design processes, seeking to destabilise the seeming constancy of simulation data. Here the term 'projective' takes on a dual meaning: it involves the literal projection of digital imagery on to physical surfaces, but in the psychological sense implies the intuitive projection of one's own desires onto the changing environment.

Bess Krietemeyer,
Design proposal
for an interactive
building facade
with electroactive
polymers, Center
for Architecture
Science and Ecology
(CASE), Rensselaer
Polytechnic
Institute, New York,
2012

Inhabitants of interactive
architectural facades
can adjust local material
behaviours, enabling
high levels of personal
customisation, environmental
comfort, and visual
communication with the
immediate context.

In his book *The Projective Cast* (1995), architect, teacher and historian Robin Evans questions the stolid relationship between geometry and architecture, investigating the ambiguities of projection and the interaction of imagination with projection. He writes: 'What connects thinking to imagination, imagination to drawing, drawing to building, and buildings to our eyes is projection in one guise or another, or processes that we have chosen to model on projection.'[1] In this way, the investigative territories of these experiments are not merely the laboratory and the simulated environments they project, but the 'zones of the instability',[2] which Evans locates at the transmissional intersection of projection and imagination. The hybrid-reality tools developed in the ongoing research at Syracuse ultimately seek to cultivate these zones to establish a co-creative sense of projective empowerment for users.

Bess Krietemeyer and Lorne Covington/ NOIRFLUX, Augmented reality dynamic facade simulation, Interactive Design and Visualization Lab (IDVL), Syracuse Center of Excellence, Syracuse University, New York, 2016

Large-scale interactive projections at the IDVL simulate an electroactive facade's dynamic material behaviours as a user changes position or gestures in the space. An analysis of the resulting solar insolation is updated in real time to visualise the relationship between occupant control, facade appearance and energy performance.

Projective Design Processes

Environmental data provides a tremendous opportunity for designers and city planners to evaluate existing and predicted urban performance across many dimensions. The use of data from various sources such as web feeds, geospatial information, census records and smartphones is becoming progressively used within city governments for improvements in public transit, waste management, green space and public safety, among others. Environmental data is being linked to the quality of urban life through simulation tools that evaluate the impact of urban design on issues such as walkability and building energy use.[3] In an effort to bring together new users and datasets, interactive urban modelling tools are being developed to create data-driven 3D urban observatories and urban decision-support systems designed for non-expert stakeholders in city development.[4] The exploration of shared interactive platforms for real-time design and data feedback can be seen in experiments such as the open-source CityScope at the MIT Media Lab[5] and the Collaborative Tangible Interface (CoTI) at the Center of Complex Engineering Systems at the King Abdulaziz City for Science and Technology (KACST) and MIT.[6]

These platforms provide an effective means for communicating and testing the impact of multiple design proposals with key stakeholders during the decision-making process from a top-down city-planning perspective. However, the complex exchange between the human body and bioclimatic energy flows in the context of architectural and urban design has yet to be fully understood from the perspective of the end user. It is difficult to predict how people will behave in proposed design solutions, yet they are important players in how a built environment truly performs. End users are not typically involved in the energy analysis and design decision-making processes, nor are they exposed to it, despite being a valuable source of first-hand experiences, preferences and desires. Excluding them from the design decision-making process is a missed opportunity if not a critical misstep.

art of the lack of end-user involvement is due to the proprietary nature of the information being analysed or proposed, but also to the seemingly cryptic characteristics of the environmental data that can drive a design decision. Energy simulation results and their visualisations, though powerful tools for objective design optimisation, are not intuitive to understand for most people, and architects and engineers often misinterpret simulation results. Even when well understood, the representation of these results typically privileges the designer's perspective, or it focuses on quantifiable scales of analysis rather than more qualitative and holistic views. Results are often displayed as static snapshots of a complex dynamic condition, which also makes it difficult to view different perspectives or to update design changes in real time.

How can we perceive and experience our built environment in new ways to better understand the energetic relationships between our bodies, buildings and cities? How can design and visualisation environments empower a wider audience with knowledge and opportunities for engagement in design decision-making processes?

Bess Krietemeyer and Lorne Covington/ NOIRFLUX, Augmented projection and virtual reality tools for design, Interactive Design and Visualization Lab (IDVL), Syracuse Center of Excellence, Syracuse University, New York, 2015

Wearers of the virtual-reality head-mounted display can experience a fully immersive environment of interactive architectural systems such as the dynamic electroactive facade. Gestural and position tracking enable virtual interaction within the simulation, while the stereoscopic view is simultaneously projected at full scale beyond.

The research team is developing interactive visualisation and simulation methods that enable designers, researchers and end users to experience and shape the aesthetic and energetic characteristics of buildings and their urban environments.

Hybrid-Reality Design

These questions of scale, real-time energy feedback and end-user experience are being explored at the IDVL in a series of ongoing experiments. With students from various departments at Syracuse University, the research team is developing interactive visualisation and simulation methods that enable designers, researchers and end users to experience and shape the aesthetic and energetic characteristics of buildings and their urban environments. The multidisciplinary team challenges presumed bounded knowledge spaces of research by bringing distinct skill sets and perspectives to the experimentation, in turn shaping new co-design processes of innovation.

Through a combination of hybrid-reality visualisation and energy-analysis techniques, interactive design software by NOIRFLUX is being linked with environmental sensors and instrumented data to virtually experience dynamic city flows and to simulate the performance of future design proposals at both building and urban scales. The broader objectives are threefold: to visualise the energetic principles and impact of the design of the built environment; to provide more intuitive perspectives of data at localised levels for educators, researchers and the general public; and to empower end users with knowledge to engage in design decision-making.

The IDVL provides an experimental platform for exploring these objectives from different perspectives and across multiple scales. At the scale of the building facade, the Lab provides a space for viewing an augmented- and virtual-reality simulation of interactive architectural facade materials through a first-person perspective. Materials such as electroactive or thermochromic shape-memory polymers that are being developed for high-performance facades have the capacity to mediate environmental flows while catering to the individual demands of a building's inhabitants. For example, a thermally active microfluidic pumping mechanism being developed at Syracuse University,[7] and an electro-responsive facade being prototyped at the Center for Architecture Science and Ecology (CASE) at Rensselaer Polytechnic Institute, both have the potential to address individual desires for localised views, daylight or privacy, while simultaneously blocking unwanted solar heat gain.[8] These experiments require unconventional modes of visualisation to understand how their extreme flexibility and immediate customisability impact individual and collective behaviour, environmental performance and architectural decision-making.

Using floor-to-ceiling projection, infrared sensors, virtual-reality devices and gestural tracking techniques, the IDVL team has developed hybrid-reality simulations to visualise and quantify the multidimensional performance effects of these systems. This allows for rapid iterative design and testing of interactive architectural assemblies that are otherwise too expensive to physically prototype in their current phase of development. As a result of the interactive visualisations, design discoveries at the larger virtual scale can inform the development of the material system itself. Moreover, the large-scale interactive visual environment is available for researchers and visitors at SyracuseCoE to view, experience and provide feedback. In turn, the variable preferences of users introduce unanticipated contingencies into the design of the system.

The visualisations from a first-person perspective enable a more intuitive understanding of abstract design concepts and performance data, thus reducing miscommunication of design intentions, which are not often clearly conveyed between disciplines. A shared and accessible visualisation space for collaborative innovation opens the door for engaging audiences that extend beyond academic boundaries. This unlocks the process for those who do not usually use conventional architectural tools, but are equally if not more invested in discovering design solutions for their local built environment.

Bess Krietemeyer, Amber Bartosh and Lorne Covington/ NOIRFLUX, First-person perspective simulation, Interactive Design and Visualization Lab (IDVL), Syracuse Center of Excellence, Syracuse University, New York, 2016

Street-level views of an urban-scale energy analysis allow viewers to experience the bioclimatic data visualisation of solar radiation at the local human scale from a first-person perspective. Multiple viewers can gesturally navigate the downtown area to view different microclimates within the city.

Bess Krietemeyer and
Lorne Covington/
NOIRFLUX, Interactive
facade simulation,
Interactive Design
and Visualization
Lab (IDVL), Syracuse
Center of Excellence,
Syracuse University,
New York, 2016

Individual position-tracking
and gestural body motions
trigger immediate responses
from the interactive
facade simulation, such as
customisable patterns and
local openings for views and
daylight.

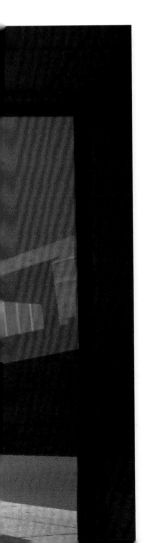

Projective Urban Design Laboratory

An accessible, multi-user design platform that emphasises
the end user's perspective of the built environment demands
exposure and input from the very people who will experience it.
How can everyday users virtually inhabit local dynamic energy
flows and contribute to a dialogue on the future design and
performance of their own buildings and cities? The techniques
of the IDVL were transferred into a public and interactive
media projection installation at MoST, as part of the museum's
permanent exhibit 'Energy: Powering Our Future'. Here, the IDVL
team's public platform establishes a 'projective urban design
laboratory', setting the stage for an open dialogue between
community stakeholders and professional designers, and
engaging a wider audience in making energy flows specific to
their locale visible.

Using similar hybrid-reality visualisation and energy-analysis
techniques developed at the IDVL, the MoST exhibit performs as
a projective living laboratory for the city. Multiple perspectives of
temporal bioclimatic data visualisations can be projected through
a dynamic and interactive augmented-reality surface. Visitors
can virtually fly overhead for a holistic view of solar radiation
patterns, or dive into the city streets to immerse themselves in
local ambient flows updated in real time. A 3D projection map of
the bioclimatic data onto a scaled physical model accompanies
the first-person experience to simultaneously provide a
navigational key through gestural interaction, which allows all
viewers to participate in the action collectively.

Visitors can interact with and receive real-time feedback on design decisions, whether through modifying building materials, redirecting waste heat of buildings or experimenting with architectural design proposals to visualise resulting ambient energy flows. Educational workshops for creating DIY weather stations enable all ages to curate and collect their own data for the projective urban design laboratory.

A live-streaming data visualisation of the projective urban design laboratory that includes visitor activity and their perceptual views of the city is simultaneously projected remotely at the IDVL at the SyracuseCoE (located about a mile from the museum). Here, anonymous user point-cloud data can be gathered to observe the frequency and range of gestural actions used to navigate the simulations. This provides a lens with which to investigate patterns of use and the role of first-person perspective in interpreting bioclimatic information and its interface with users and the surrounding architectural context.

Anonymous user point-cloud data can be gathered to observe the frequency and range of gestural actions used to navigate the simulations.

ss Krietemeyer, Amber Bartosh
d Lorne Covington/NOIRFLUX,
mputational hybrid-reality model,
teractive Design and Visualization
b (IDVL), Syracuse Center of
cellence, Syracuse University,
w York, 2016

combined augmented-reality wall with projection
apping onto a physical model provides an
eractive public platform for visitors to interact
th and experience dynamic and ambient energy
ws at multiple scales within their city. Users can
sturally navigate the model to locate specific
rspectives and views of how the city performs
multiple levels, as well as how their presence
pacts that performance locally.

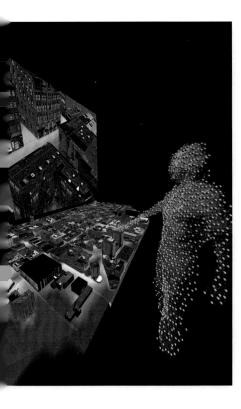

Bess Krietemeyer and
Lorne Covington/
NOIRFLUX, Point-
cloud data of
museum visitors,
Interactive Design
and Visualization
Lab (IDVL), Syracuse
Center of Excellence,
Syracuse University,
New York, 2016

A multi-sensor system tracks
museum visitors within the
projection urban laboratory
exhibition boundaries using
point-cloud data. Patterns of
use can be observed at the
IDVL for improving how end
users perceive and interpret
energy data as well as how
they navigate their local urban
environments.

Empowering Audiences

Experiments with the projective installation open a dialogue between designers, stakeholders and end users about design ideas, diverse interests and common goals. The hybrid-reality tools, whether developed in the Lab or as part of a museum exhibit, demonstrate the communicative potential of multiscalar and interactive visualisations to engage a wider, more public audience. The projective urban design laboratory arms people with knowledge to take part in decision-making that informs future urban revitalisation activities, thus promoting an awareness of users' needs and interests through participatory architectural design.

Exposing the process of interaction and design in a public setting can have a profound influence on the behaviour of both designers and end users, where projective desires become part of the library of open-source data, and thus the design process. This not only allows for a more diverse set of possible outcomes, but also holds more people accountable for design decisions that impact entire communities. The physical and mental projections involved in the process destabilise the seeming stability of quantitative energy data, resulting in imaginative urban configurations. By providing designers, researchers and end users with capabilities to engage with architectural design proposals to visualise relationships between ambient energy flows and the designed environment, the capacity of simulation modelling is expanded by empowering a wider audience to better understand their local ecologies and to co-construct sustainable design ideas. This enables the community to actively participate in the making of their environments both bioclimatically and symbolically. ⌂

Notes
1. Robin Evans, *The Projective Cast*, MIT Press (Cambridge, MA), 1995, p xxxi.
2. *Ibid*, p xxxi.
3. Christoph F Reinhart *et al*, 'Umi – An Urban Simulation Environment for Building Energy Use, Daylighting and Walkability', *Proceedings of BS2013: 13th Conference of the International Building Performance Simulation Association*, Chambéry, France, 26–28 August 2013.
4. The President's Council of Advisors on Science and Technology (PCAST), 'Report To The President: Technology and the Future of Cities', February 2016, p 73: www.whitehouse.gov/sites/whitehouse.gov/files/images/Blog/PCAST%20Cities%20Report%20_%20FINAL.pdf.
5. Urban Intervention Simulation: http://cp.media.mit.edu/city-simulation.
6. Salma Aldawood *et al*, 'Collaborative Tangible Interface (CoTI) for Complex Decision Support Systems', in Aaron Marcus (ed), *Design, User Experience, and Usability: Users and Interactions*, Springer International Publishing (Los Angeles, CA), 2015, pp 415–24.
7. Jaimee M Robertson *et al*, 'Thermally Driven Microfluidic Pumping via Reversible Shape Memory Polymers', *Smart Materials and Structures*, 25 (8), August 2016, pp 85043–56.
8. Bess Krietemeyer, Brandon Andow and Anna Dyson, 'A Computational Design Framework Supporting Human Interaction with Environmentally-Responsive Building Envelopes', *International Journal of Architectural Computing*, 13 (1), 2015, pp 1–24.

**Claudia Pasquero
and Marco Poletto**

ecoLogicStudio, Solana
Open Aviary, Ulcinj,
Montenegro,
2016

View of salt crusts on the Solana
Ulcinj; the image shows one of
the abandoned ponds in the fina
stages of the salt production
process.

ecoLogicStudio's Solana Open Aviary in Ulcinj, Montenegro

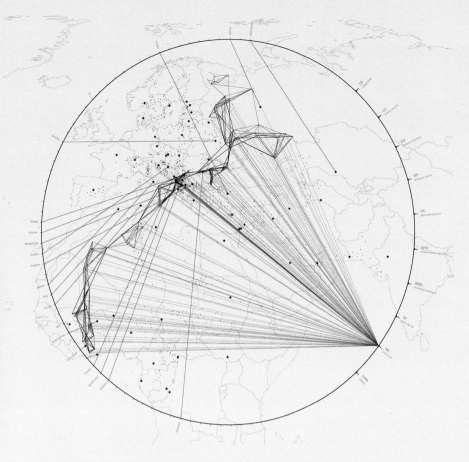

Intercontinental plan of the transnational network of birds' nesting locations of the Open Aviary, proposed as an interface updated in real time through satellite mapping and live feeds from bird tracking devices.

tal

gn

ows

Artificial landscapes whose human use has expired pose a major reprogramming challenge. The Solana Open Aviary, a transformation of former salt marshes into an enormous open-air ornithological park, shows how cutting-edge technology can be used to address biopolitical, operational and tectonic concerns in such situations. **Claudia Pasquero and Marco Poletto** – cofounders of the project-leading London practice ecoLogicStudio – explain.

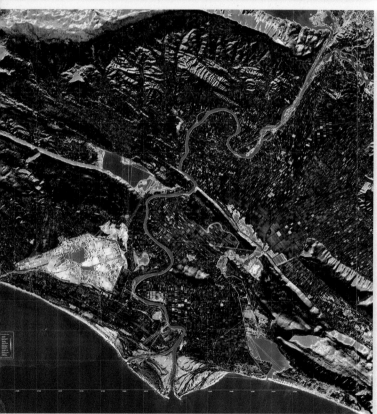

top: Infrared satellite depiction of the Bojana-Buna Delta region, underlining the new definition of habitat as an extended operational field pursued as part of this biodigital design proposal.

above: The operational field of the Bojana-Buna region computed by the normalised difference water index (NDWI) algorithm to evidence degrees of wetness and the relationship to the local networks of bird nesting sites.

In the age of the Anthropocene, no territory is left untouched by human influence. Notions of wilderness and environmental conservation have to be reassessed against the new milieu of planetary urbanisation. Over the last 10 years ecoLogicStudio has developed a biodigital design workflow as an operative tool to conceive and design augmented territories and ecosystemic architectures for which human inhabitation is understood as a co-evolutionary force of natural ecosystems.

In the now established tradition of practice-driven research ecoLogicStudio's experimental design activity has progressed under the impulse of direct engagement with real contexts and design briefs as well as through collaboration with academic and design institutions. One extraordinary project that the firm has become involved in is the transformation of the Solana Ulcinj in Montenegro. The project is the brainchild of architect Diana Vucinic of the Montenegro Ministry of Tourism and Sustainable Development, with Professor Bart Lootsma (University of Innsbruck) and Katharina Weinberger (architecturaltheory.eu) as curators of the Montenegro Pavilion at the Venice Architecture Biennale 2016 where it was first presented. The Pavilion featured four project proposals, one of which – the Solana Open Aviary – was realised by ecoLogicStudio.

With a surface area of 14.9 square kilometres (5.8 square miles), Solana is one of the largest salt marshes in the Mediterranean region, a man-made landscape created in the late 1920s which has come to be regarded as an exceptional biotope of local, national and global importance. Since the decline of salt production as a viable activity in the Mediterranean, it has become critical to find new models to re-programme coastal artificial landscapes such as this, by enhancing their touristic and cultural value as ornithological parks and articulating their new-found interest as marine resorts. The Solana Ulcinj project was conceived as a challenge to 'come up with new proposals for saving the important ecological condition of the Solana Ulcinj and the unique cultural qualities of its landscape, while at the same time enabling and regulating economic interests in the area', explained Lootsma and Weinberger in their brief.

Given the complexity of re-programming such a large territory and under the premises of practice-based research, ecoLogicStudio (Marco Poletto and Claudia Pasquero with the assistance of Terezia Greskova and Vlad Daraban) teamed up with three research partners: the Urban Morphogenesis Lab (research team: Claudia Pasquero, Maj Plemenitas and Stuart Maggs) at the Bartlett School of Architecture, University College London (UCL); the European Space Agency (ESA) research group based in Rome (led by director of research, Pier Giorgio Marchetti); and Aarhus School of Architecture (lead researcher: Marco Poletto). Responding to the specificities of a brief so engrained into notions of artificial ecology and infrastructural landscape, the work of ecoLogicStudio began by uncovering, measuring and evaluating the latent potentials in the Bojana-Buna Delta region, which includes the area occupied by the Solana.

The ambition was to propose a method and related workflow to productively develop a series of pilot projects capable of a catalytic action at multiple scales.

ecoLogicStudio's intervention focused on the generation an urban co-action plan, with a logic of co-evolution natural and artificial systems. The plan frames the site through managerial zones at different resolutions: molecular, focusing on photosynthetic bacterial ecologies in the Solana's salt crust and brine; architectural, looking at the Solana's local ecology in relationship with its machines and water flow regulating devices; and global, concerning networks and behaviours of migrating birds. It became clear from this analysis, furthered through site visits in spring 2016, that social disconnection between urban development and the understanding of the local landscape was taking place, with evident negative repercussions for both realms. As a consequence, ecoLogicStudio's proposal developed into the notion of Open Aviary, as a means to stimulate reconnection and intensify co-action between socioeconomic groups and their immediate surrounding landscape.

This key design concept of the Open Aviary is inspired by the possibility of digitally tracking and simulating global migratory fluxes of birds and promoting the emergence of a new concept of natural reserve as a boundless, open and networked man-made ecosystem. The conditions of the artificial territory formerly occupied by the salt production plant make the context ideal for the actualisation of this concept, into what would be the world's first Open Aviary, an augmented ornithological park where people can study, experience and affect the co-evolution of humans and birds.

On site the proposed Open Aviary will be quite literally an aviary without a net, where birds and humans explore close interaction without being forcefully enclosed in a confined envelope. This is made possible by a carefully designed workflow managing the flows of information, matter and energy provided by the deployment of digital bird tracking technologies, high-resolution satellite earth monitoring and robotically driven land 3D scanning/sculpting. ecoLogicStudio's integrated design of digital technologies and landscape ecology confers multiple meanings on the word 'open', both in the physical and virtual realms: an open-source ornithological database, open networks of migratory sites and open systems habitat.

left: Developed as a speculative biodigital design, the Solana Open Aviary is conceived as part of a larger networked city incorporating existing informal settlements and water infrastructures while introducing new pedestrian and cycling links, renewable energy infrastructures and ornithological sites.

below: As part of the biodigital proposal, architectures for birds to nest or rest were designed to increase artificial habitat articulation and human–bird interaction.

Through intradisciplinary design the project embraces the implications of its concept at all scales, from the intercontinental to the molecular. The three main levels are, firstly, the biopolitics of the Open Aviary – a biopolitical simulation at the intercontinental scale describing how habitats across many different countries and regions are in fact part of a single project when it comes to preserving the global bird population and their complex migrating behaviours. Secondly, the operational field of the Open Aviary is facilitated by a satellite-enabled survey at the regional scale, carried out in partnership with ESA. Through the eye of Sentinella-2, ESA's new high-resolution earth-monitoring satellite, the Open Aviary embodies never-before-seen detailed scanning of biochemical processes on the ground and water, revealing a landscape that is inextricably the product of the combined action of human agency and technology with local biological life.

The third level of the project's intradisciplinary design is the tectonic of the Open Aviary, a robotically fabricated artificial landscape that enables a new life for the salt marsh and its infrastructure in the biodigital age. Using local materials, such as the unique black clay mud and the salt crystals, an open process of natural mineral accretion is iteratively 3D scanned, accelerated and articulated to evolve a highly differentiated landscape capable of attracting a wider variety of bird species present in the region and accommodate multiple architectural programmes – from research to sport/leisure and healthcare.

To articulate these three levels of the project, ecoLogicStudio collaborated very closely with its main research partners. Combining forces with the Urban Morphogenesis Lab at the Bartlett, UCL, the practice was able to interface with ESA in Rome to define a workflow enabling the team to design with near-real-time data from their new Sentinella-2 satellite. ESA provided the Lab with a set of virtual machines (VMs) from which Level-1 data were downloaded, averaged in pixels each representing an area on the surface of the earth of 10 by 10 metres (roughly 33 by 33 feet). Dedicated software installed on the VMs enabled the processing of those datasets with three kinds of algorithms, to produce a set of false colour images that were called infrared, normalised water and vegetation indexes. These images and their datasets were input into ecoLogicStudio's design simulation workflows, mainly developed within the Grasshopper® platform from McNeel. Such a workflow also enables direct communication with machines for both 3D printing and on-site robotic actuation.

The sensors on the new Sentinella-2 satellite are capable of detecting biochemical processes in the project site as well as pollutants, and of distinguishing between multiple species of plants and soils. Such an unprecedented level of detail has enabled a redefinition of the notion of habitat, as depicted by the operational field maps: an operational concept of habitat is essential to the idea of the Open Aviary, where the terrain becomes co-evolutionary with its inhabiting forces, be they human or non-human. The result is what ecoLogicStudio

Biodigital design proposal to reprogramme a coastal man-made saline wetland as an ornithological park. The manufactured landscape of local black clay and salt accretions is robotically fabricated in real time in response to seasonal fluctuations of birds' global migration pattern.

efines as in-human landscape or architecture, coproduced y human and non-human forces and therefore emerging as new ontological object.

This is a shift in perspective enabled by the specific esearch strategy that ecoLogicStudio has adopted, and in e conception of robotically enabled landscapes, for which atural processes such as mineral accretion – typical of etland, salt lakes and salt marshes – are accelerated and igitally manipulated to enable the emergence of novel norphologies. These biodigital material systems conjure ossible scenarios to manufacture an adaptive substratum for ne Open Aviary to host both human and aviary programmes n the near future. Ultimately a real-time feedback between emote sensing and on-site intervention in the landscape etermines the morphogenesis of the Solana Open Aviary, which is shaped by the dialogue between natural and artificial, local and global ecologies.

This strategy also actualises the interfacing of multiple urveillance mechanisms and proposes their fruition as open-ource databases of knowledge. Satellite monitoring, drone D scanning and ornithologists' fieldwork are interfaced and nform each other, promoting a new form of citizen science

whereby both locals and tourists become actively engaged in the process of understanding as well as transforming the Solana Open Aviary. The ecoLogicStudio team believes that such an approach constitutes a powerful response to some of the most urgent problems affecting the site, such as poaching, which is currently driving down the number of protected birds in the area, and uncontrolled development occurring primarily on the strip of land dividing the Solana from the Mediterranean Sea.

The protection and conservation of the Solana Ulcinj's cultural identity as an infrastructural landscape and its ecosystemic value as an ornithological park is achieved through the opening and the hyper-articulation of its boundaries, as illustrated by the 3D-printed study models exhibited at the Montenegro Pavilion during the Venice Biennale of Architecture 2016. Increasing habitat articulation, informational exchange and network connectivity make the Open Aviary a more resilient system, one that is inherently adaptive and receptive to future change. The Solana Open Aviary is also an example of the future articulation of the Urbansphere, the global apparatus of contemporary urbanity. ⌂

ght and bottom: High-solution 3D-printed ylon model of an Open viary architecture, emonstrating the material ffect of bird flocking mulated morphologies.

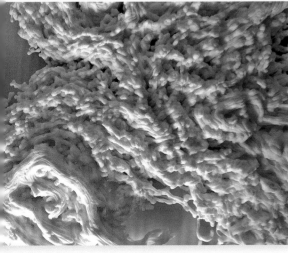

Martijn de Waal,
Michiel de Lange
and
Matthijs Bouw

The Hackable City ■

Can computer hacking have positive parallels in the shaping of the built environment? The Hackable City research project was set up with this question in mind, to investigate the potential of digital platforms to open up the citymaking process. Its cofounders **Martijn de Waal,**

One Architecture,
The Mobile City Foundation,
Delva Landscape Architects,
Studioninedots and
Stadslab Buiksloterham,
Hackable Cityplot,
Amsterdam,
2016

Due to the economic crisis, the
redevelopment of the brownfield site
of Buiksloterham in Amsterdam Noord
was opened up to new actors such
as self-builders and building groups.
They have set up a coalition with larger
institutional players to develop the area
in a networked way, according to the
principles of the circular economy.

Citymaking in a Platform Society

Michiel de Lange and Matthijs Bouw here outline
the tendencies that their studies of collaborative
urban development initiatives around the world
have revealed, and ask whether knowledge
sharing and incremental change might be a better
way forward than top-down masterplans.

The rise of a broad variety of digital media platforms – from Airbnb to Uber and from local community websites to worldwide operating social media companies such as Facebook – is bringing about a platform society: one in which social and economic relations are increasingly mediated through an ecosystem of interconnected digital media platforms.[1] An important impact of these platforms lies on the level of the 'hyperlocal', as they enable citizens to organise themselves into publics around local issues, and thus to act upon these issues. However, these platforms are not neutral mediators, simply linking up demand and supply in a number of social and economic domains. Contrary to rhetoric denoting them as mere connectors, it could be argued that they embody a particular ideology, or – in relation to urbanism – a particular urban imaginary and redistribution of power in practices of citymaking.

The Hackable City research project – led by cofounders One Architecture and the Mobile City Foundation, and currently carried out in cooperation with the Amsterdam University of Applied Sciences, the University of Amsterdam and Utrecht University – has since 2012 introduced the notion of the 'hackable city' as a lens to understand the role these platforms play in the processes of citymaking. The notion is used to ask how digital media can be employed to open up urban institutions and infrastructures to systemic change in the public interest. As such it explores the opportunities these platforms offer for modes of collaborative citymaking that empower (hyper)local stakeholders in an open and democratic society.

The success of cities partially lies in the fact that they are open platforms.

Hackable Cities: Open or Closed Technological Constructs?

The term 'hackable city' is a productive one for three different reasons. Firstly, the term 'hacking' directly refers to engagement with computer systems or networks, and foregrounds the use of digital technologies in the process of citymaking. Specifically, hacking is defined as the processes of opening up these existing systems or networks to playfully reappropriate technologies beyond their intended designs. As such it can be understood both as a practice – the act of appropriation – and as an affordance of a system – to what extent does it enable that appropriation to be carried out easily?

All kinds of urban practices that use the physical city as an interface to connect citizens with one another are now partly remediated through online platforms. Whether it is hailing a taxi in the street, buying a book in a local bookshop, or finding a date in a bar or club, as a popular advertisement has put it: 'there's an app for that'. These apps are often integrated in a larger ecosystem based on the collection of user data and the referral of consumers to particular services. Similarly, many new platforms such as Nextdoor.com have emerged that allow citizens in neighbourhoods to exchange services, ideas and resources.

In relation to practices of citymaking, the role of these platforms and a good understanding of their workings are important. The Spanish sociologist Manuel Castells has made the point that cities themselves can be understood as 'platforms', or 'material interfaces' that connect individual city dwellers with collective practices, experiences and rhythms.[2] To put it in the words of the American architecture critic Paul Goldberger, cities could even be understood as 'the original internet', as 'random connections are what make them work, and surprise and a sense of infinite choice is what gives them their power'.[3]

In other words, the success of cities partially lies in the fact that they are open platforms. Within the urban fabric, citizens can create their own sites of exchange, and an urban public sphere comes into being when all of these interactions start overlapping spatially. That is also when all kinds of new connections can be forged. In the terminology of this article cities can be 'hacked' or appropriated by their citizens. Of course, not all citizens have the same means or power to do so, and there are huge inequalities that need to be addressed. Not all cities are equally open for appropriation. Yet even in cities in closed political systems, citizens may still find a place to voice their dissent, or organise a shadow economy.

Talking about the city in terms of hackability means foregrounding the question of the extent to which urban spaces and practices can still be opened up, made legible and understandable and appropriated beyond their intended designs. Like hackers do, it should be possible to 'unblackbox' the digital media platforms that have started to play a prominent part in our lives, and come to a better understanding of their underlying logic. To what extent can these new platforms be opened up by citizens? Who has access to the data they aggregate, under what conditions? Who governs these platforms and decides on the rules that are encoded in their algorithms? Hacking as a lens brings these questions to the fore in the debate on the role of platforms in the process of citymaking.

Hackable Cities as an Alternative Urban Imaginary

There is a second reason why hacking is a useful term to talk about the future of cities. The notion of hacking and the various computer-centred hacker cultures that have emerged in the last half a century can also be invoked as an alternative imaginary. In this case, hacking is invoked as a particular normative ethos that could guide the design or regulation of digital media platforms. There is not such a thing as a singular hacker culture, and its popular understandings have ranged from criminal practices such as breaking into computer systems and credit card fraud to more positive connotations that centre on collaboration towards a common public good – as found, for instance, in the open-source software movement.

Urbego and Micromega (Mara Papavasileiou and Alexandros Zomas), Akalyptos 2.0: an urban pocket methodology implementation, Athens, 2016

In Athens most apartment buildings (*polykatoikia*) have an underused backyard within the interior of the urban block, called the *akalyptos* (literally: the uncovered).

The network of Urbego and Micromega, as local partners, propose a methodology of participatory design to combine and reclaim these left-over spaces as collectively managed shared spaces.

The first understanding reminds us that we should never be too naive about computer networks, privacy and security, and that all systems may indeed be hacked by contrarian forces. The second gives us an outlook on citymaking that makes use of technology to work towards a public good. For instance, we find such an outlook in American author Anthony M Townsend's description of 'civic hackers'. In his book *Smart Cities: Big Data, Civic Hackers, and the Quest for a New Utopia* (2013) he describes civic hackers as citizens who do not buy into the dominant smart city myths, but instead organise their own decentralised networks of online collaboration, for instance through the organisation of hackathons.[4]

A number of characteristics can be traced in these kinds of descriptions of hackers' practices, referring to various instances of hacker cultures. First, hacking is about learning by doing, sharing knowledge and learning from each other. Often, hacker cultures also revolve around collaborating towards a common goal. Think of examples such as the open software movement, or the culture of sharing knowledge around an online phenomenon like Wikipedia. Next, hacking is also about a process of tinkering, trying things out through small incremental changes, rather than by creating top-down masterplans. Can such principles of learning from each other and collaboration towards a common good be transferred to citymaking? And how can online platforms stimulate these kinds of practices? The notion of hacking can bring out particular qualities found in hacker cultures that revolve around collaboration towards a common good, and as such function as an alternative urban imaginary to be invoked in practices of citymaking.

To get a better grasp of what this imaginary of the hackable city could look like, the eponymous project has so far conducted two studies of collaborative citymaking initiatives. In 2013 and 2014 the team mapped 84 projects in Amsterdam, and analysed 8 of these in more depth. In 2016 similar analyses were carried out on a broad range of projects in an international context, including Athens, São Paulo and Shenzhen.

In São Paulo, the team uncovered many examples of initiatives that aimed to reactivate public spaces, varying in scope from a citizen-led movement that started programming events at the Largo da Batata public square and decorated it with new urban furniture, to the online platform project Pracas.com.br, that provides tools for communities to set the agenda for, and to coordinate action around, the renovation of local squares. In Athens, the team analysed projects like Traces of Commerce, which reactivated a vacant shopping arcade by inviting social entrepreneurs to take residency and organise public workshops. Another example in Athens was Akalyptos 2.0, a project that through a procedure of co-design aims to pool the underused open spaces of apartment blocks in the city into a shared courtyard. In Amsterdam, The Hackable City's current research has focused on the development of Buiksloterham, a brownfield site that, due to the economic crisis, was opened up to new types of urban developers such as self-builders and communal building groups. Here the chief interest lies in the dynamics of the networks they have organised to learn from each other, pool resources and collaborate to develop the area according to the logic of the circular economy.

Haris Biskos
(Potemkin) and
Martha Giannakopoulou
(If_Untitled
Architecture) Traces
of Commerce,
Athens,
2016

Due to the financial crisis,
Athens has seen many vacant
commercial spaces such as
this Stoa Empoton (Arcade of
Merchants).

What The Hackable City's investigations have uncovered is that many of these projects follow a path of seven steps. They start with the definition of an issue by an involved stakeholder. From the perspective of hackability, here an important question is: who has the power and the means to name an issue and put it on the agenda? Next, attempts are made to visualise or communicate the issue at hand, both through online campaigns and by manifestations in public space. Tactics are then employed to engage a public around the issue. In the next phase this public is given a platform to convene. This could again take the shape of an online platform, varying from a Facebook group to a purpose-built platform. Here an important question is the issue of how the public is represented on this platform. Are members represented as individuals, or as an aggregated collective voice? How are individuals represented? Can people contribute anonymously, or only with their real names? Are external protocols used – such as Facebook profiles – and what happens with the data that is generated?

These platforms lead to the next phases: usually tools are introduced through which publics can ideate, learn and exchange upon the issue, and consequently pool resources or act upon it. In the seventh and last phase, actors involved start looking for ways to institutionalise temporary interventions, proposals or solutions. How can the results of the whole process lead to a lasting outcome? This is not always necessary or even desirable, but often the goal of hackable projects is indeed to contribute to a more systemic change, rather than producing a one-off event.

Alongside this cycle of seven steps, The Hackable City's research has additionally found that many initiatives make use of a number of particular 'tools' or 'strategies' that can also be seen as the building stones of 'hackable city' projects. For instance, many projects have constructed 'knowledge communities'. These are platforms through which participants can learn from each other. They can take the form of wikis, weblogs or informal meet-ups in which participants exchange knowledge and insights. Another important strategy is 'trust brokering': before a public can act on a particular issue, its participants need to be able to trust each other. Whereas many digital media platforms here rely on online reputation systems and user reviews, the Hackable City team found that many of the initiatives they investigated tend instead to use social events as the most important way to built up trust. A last example of one of the strategies used is capacity building: many of the projects researched undertake efforts to educate their participants, getting them up to speed with new skill sets that can help them to act.

The Hackable City,
The Hackable City process,
2015

'Hackable city' initiatives usually evolve through seven phases, from the naming of an issue to the institutionalisation of a particular approach to address that issue.

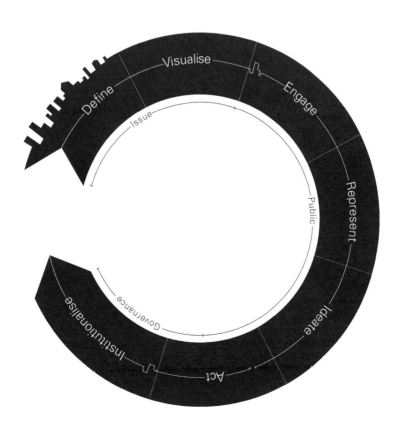

The Hackable City as a Critical Lens

A third application of the term 'hacking' is found in its usefulness as a critical lens. Whereas the hacker ethos can indeed empower citizens to collaboratively set goals and work towards them, it is necessary also to turn a critical eye to these practices. In reality cities are also sites of contestation, where different groups of citizens may have different preferences or economic interests, and where existing power relations do not all of a sudden disappear with the emergence of collaborative digital media platforms.

Conflicts may arise between the public interest at large and the interests of smaller groups of citizens. How does the agency that individuals may gain from a hackable city perspective hold up to existing practices of democratic decision making? What is the legitimacy of hacks proposed by newly empowered collectives? In the Netherlands, the social scientists Evelien Tonkens, Margo Trappenburg, Menno Hurenkamp and Jante Schmidt have recently pointed out that an approach to citymaking that makes more room for self-organisation and bottom-up initiatives may work especially well for those who have the skills and political connections to get their 'hacks' off the ground – while others without the energy, the skills or the willingness to participate may be left behind.[5] The notion of hacking as a skill set, and as practices that serve collective but not necessarily public interests, brings these aspects to the fore.

In the course of The Hackable City's research, this perspective has led to the development of another heuristic model used to understand and to map practices of collaborative citymaking and their relations to democratic institutions. On the left-hand side of the model are individual citizens. The majority of 'hackable city' projects aim to organise individuals in some form of a collective, as indicated in the centre of the model. In most instances, individual citizens contribute some form of resources to the collective, be it time, money, knowledge or materials. In return they receive a product or service, like a better public space, locally produced energy, or a house that is the result of a collaborative building group.

However, these collectives do not operate in a vacuum. They operate within legal, regulatory, economic and social frameworks set by local institutions, as illustrated on the right-hand side of the model. It is these democratically elected or controlled institutions that have the legitimacy to establish public interests and come up with policy instruments to safeguard those interests. As British urbanist Dan Hill has recently pointed out, there is a potential conflict between the two sides of the diagram.[6] The left side is the 'social' where citizens collaborate towards common goals. The right could be understood as the 'democratic', the institutions through which we govern our cities. In a European social democratic tradition, these institutions have always played a central role in the safeguarding of public values in our societies. A singlehanded focus on the notion of hacking per se may undermine this tradition and favour the social practices of particular – privileged – groups.

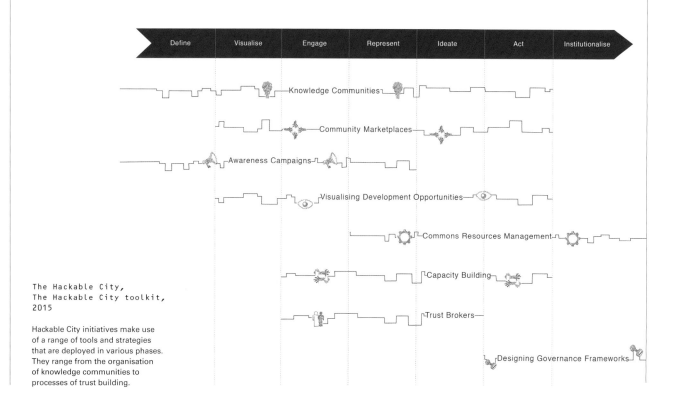

The Hackable City,
The Hackable City toolkit,
2015

Hackable City initiatives make use of a range of tools and strategies that are deployed in various phases. They range from the organisation of knowledge communities to processes of trust building.

At the same time, these social practices could contribute to public interests as well: for instance, in the reactivation of public spaces, the design of schemes for hyperlocal renewable energy production networks, or the organisation of a much more varied housing landscape than the traditional market or current regulation would allow. That is why one of the main research themes of The Hackable City lies in the question of how these practices of collective organisation can be better tuned to institutional practices and the design of instruments that could help forge this link. How can a 'hack', once it is undertaken, demonstrate its contribution to public values and convince policymakers to adopt its approach into legal and policy frameworks? Whereas the invocation of a hacker ethos may bring attention to the design and regulation of collaborative practices and platforms that would allow individuals to organise themselves as collectives around communal issues of interest, at the same time these practices somehow need to be embedded in institutional frameworks that can safeguard public interests.

It could even be argued, perhaps counterintuitively, that in a hackable city, the process of citymaking should not be left to hackers alone. Procedures of institutional democratic governance may even become more important, not less. As when room is made for hacking initiatives, institutions that are able to legitimately determine and uphold the public interest will have to play a central role. On the one hand they have to make sure that the city remains an open system, and safeguard or even promote its hackability. At the same time these institutions are the only ones who have the legitimacy to also safeguard inclusiveness and the public interest in the hackable city. ∆

Notes
1. Cristina Ampatzidou, Matthijs Bouw, Froukje van de Klundert, Michiel de Lange and Martijn de Waal, *The Hackable City: A Research Manifesto and Design Toolkit*, Amsterdam, The Knowledge Mile Publications (Amsterdam), 2015; José Van Dijck, Thomas Poell and Martijn de Waal, *De Platformsamenleving* (*The Platform Society*), forthcoming.
2. Manuel Castells, 'The Culture of Cities in the Information Age', in Ida Susser (ed), *The Castells Reader on Cities and Social Theory*, Blackwell (Malden, MA), 2002, pp 367–89.
3. Paul Goldberger, 'Cities, Place and Cyberspace', lecture held at University of California, Berkeley, 1 February 2001, http://www.paulgoldberger.com/lectures/cities-place-and-cyberspace/.
4. Anthony M Townsend, *Smart Cities: Big Data, Civic Hackers, and the Quest for a New Utopia*, WW Norton & Company (New York), 2013.
5. Evelien Tonkens, Margo Trappenburg, Menno Hurenkamp and Jante Schmidt, *Montessori democratie: Spanningen tussen burgerparticipatie en de lokale politiek*, Amsterdam University Press (Amsterdam), 2015.
6. Dan Hill, 'The Social and the Democratic, in the Social Democratic European City', Medium.com, 23 May 2016, http://bit.ly/2cROSEG.

The Hackable City, Heuristic model for the analysis and design of 'hackable cities', 2015

In a 'hackable city', individual citizens organise themselves in collectives focused around specific issues. These collectives in turn operate in legal and regulatory frameworks set by democratic institutions.

Driving the Regeneration of
Amsterdam's Amstel3 District

FROM CITIZEN PARTICIPATION TO REAL OWNERSHIP

Reinvigorating urban environments is a complex challenge involving multiple stakeholders. How can local governments and communities be enabled to work together to achieve it? **Saskia Beer** reports on ZO!City (initially named Glamourmanifest), an initiative that she founded in 2011 to transform a waning Amsterdam office district into a lively mixed-use neighbourhood. An interactive online platform is key to revealing and interlinking different parties' priorities, and has been supported by playful real-world activities to generate enthusiasm and encourage engagement.

Glamourmanifest local
community campaign launch,
Amstel3,
Amsterdam,
2011

The launch of Glamourmanifest (renamed ZO!City in 2015) – a
campaign to transform the 250-hectare (620-acre) Amstel3 office
district – was announced by posters distributed through the area.
They showed the initiator as a glamorous activist who is determined
to upgrade her daily environment with simple, low-budget tools.

Amstel3 is a 250-hectare (620-acre) office district in Amsterdam, developed in the 1980s. Positioned along major public transport hubs and motorways, it became the city's third economic cluster, accommodating more than 300 companies. However, by 2011, the area had a 27 per cent vacancy rate, which was predicted to increase due to its outdated monofunctional layout. In the economic crisis the municipality could not continue its big regeneration plans to turn Amstel3 into a lively urban neighbourhood and had to withdraw from its long-established proactive planner's role. The local market and citizens were not organised or equipped to instantly take over this role: the stakeholder network was heterogeneous and the property ownership fragmented, with 120 buildings and 80 different owners. Stakeholders had no overview and no platform to exchange ideas and take collective decisions.

Connecting Stakeholders

There was a need for the different stakeholder groups, including the municipality, to be connected and activated around Amstel3's transformation. The idea of what would become the ZO!City initiative was that everybody, from property owner to employee in one of the buildings, has something at stake in the area. By mapping those stakes and interests and identifying the overlaps, collective starting points would emerge that everybody could contribute to and benefit from. By making the first positive changes together, the potential of the area would be unveiled incrementally and the conditions and support for further interventions would be set. From talking to different people in the area, however, it became clear that most were laymen in the field of urban development and did not automatically feel called or entitled to engage in it. Many daily users had never thought about influencing their environment and assumed the municipality would not allow them to. They were not convinced about their own interest in the area and were not activated.

Campaigning for Self-Organisation

In order to put Amstel3's transformation on the local agenda as an accessible and relevant subject, a local campaign was launched in 2011, based on light-hearted storytelling with glamorous metaphors representing new qualities for Amstel3, under the name Glamourmanifest. The team organised playful actions, like flower bulb planting and pop-up champagne parties. By using social media and newsletters, communication lines were built and people's trust and enthusiasm grew.

Behind the scenes an extensive database with local demands, ambitions and supporters was developing. However, Glamourmanifest still had a centralised network structure and the small team was becoming its weakest link. A decision was taken to start focusing on helping the local community to self-organise and assume collective ownership over the transformation of their neighbourhood. In June 2015, the name Glamourmanifest was dropped in favour of ZO!City, adopting the existing local branding prefix ZO!. This move from independent agent to local platform catalysed the sense of ownership among the local businesses and property owners who had become paying members and who related to Glamourmanifest's mission, but not to its name.

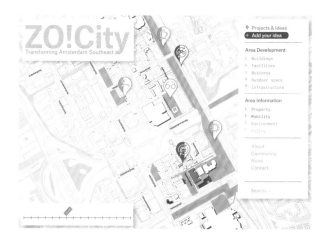

TransformCity® online dashboard,
Amsterdam pilot,
2016

top: This highly integrated and actionable online urban transformation dashboard created by ZO!City allows citizens, businesses, organisations and the government to directly exchange data and ideas and collectively plan, change and own their neighbourhood.

right: The crowdfunding infrastructure on the dashboard allows for project-based alliances to be formed and resources to be shared and combined. The rewards for engagement vary from an improvement of daily environment to real shares in local projects.

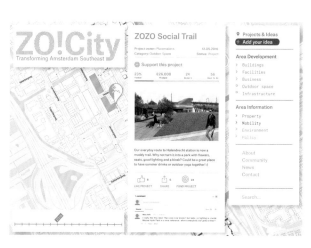

The move from independent agent to local platform catalysed the sense of ownership among the local businesses and property owners

ZO!City local community
platform future vision,
Amstel3,
Amsterdam,
2015

ZO!City was commissioned by the municipality of Amsterdam to co-create a new urban vision for the southern part of the Amstel3 district together with all stakeholders. Simple collages were used to show alternative possibilities for existing areas.

Glamourmanifest, local community mobile
cafe opening,
Amstel3, Amsterdam, 2012

Initially it was difficult for the Glamourmanifest group campaigning for the transformation of the Amstel3 district to find entrepreneurs who dared to open a cafe there. By starting with food trucks, the market potential was revived, and soon more permanent cafes opened in the area as well.

Glamourmanifest
local community
art intervention,
Amstel3,
Amsterdam,
2014

both images: Five artworks
on a large social trail near the
station offer passers-by a range
of different, coloured views
on their daily environment,
inviting them to dream about
possible alternatives for the
Amstel3 district. Intervention
in collaboration with Maxime
Vancoillie and The New
Verbalizers.

The initiative aims to deepen knowledge and experience exchange between cities, stakeholders and tools.

Urban Transformation Dashboard

The ZO!City team then set about designing and developing TransformCity, a highly integrated and actionable online urban transformation dashboard, with the help of graphic designers Bureau LUST and technical developers Systemantics. Its initial Amstel3 pilot was made financially and logistically possible by the ZO!City community of property owners and the Municipality of Amsterdam, with additional funding from the Beter Benutten Vervolg ('Optimising Use') MRA programme of the Dutch Ministry of Infrastructure and the Environment. It integrates storytelling, data sharing, co-creation, participatory democracy, crowdsourcing and crowdfunding. Its distributed network structure allows the community and the municipality to directly exchange data and ideas and collectively plan, make and own their neighbourhood. The online map shows items such as buildings, parks and stations as clickable objects that hold basic information about, for example, floor space, building year and ownership. Via the menu, detailed thematic – open and user-generated – data can be found about mobility, real estate, policy and environment.

The timeline also features recent developments and future plans and scenarios. The full interactivity makes it easy to engage directly by clicking on the map and markers, and making comments. Everybody can share their ideas and initiatives for the area; feedback is obtained both from individuals and from official institutions. With the underlying crowdfunding infrastructure, project-based alliances can be formed and resources shared and combined. Active engagement is rewarded. The first crowdfunding campaign for formalising a large social trail near the station went live during the dashboard launch in May 2016. This campaign asked for donations, offering an upgrade in daily environment in return. At the start of 2017 a campaign will go live for funding a large restaurant. In that case funders receive actual shares in the restaurant company.

During the development the local stakeholders and officials at the Amsterdam municipality were consulted about the best ways to implement the dashboard pilot in Amstel3. The municipality, excited by its new possibilities for direct interaction with the neighbourhood, is sharing data and embracing the dashboard. Property owners have uploaded building pages and many have shared their projects and ideas.

The dashboard supports ZO!City's offline activities rather than replacing them. It still takes effort to engage people and stimulate them to use the dashboard. Large groups of stakeholders can be reached and invited around the table 24/7, but inclusivity will always need attention. The plan is to continue investing in an on-site presence to make sure the overall process is adopted sustainably. The team also encounters interesting questions regarding participatory democracy that will be further explored with the municipality. When is an idea legitimate? What happens when different ideas conflict? What are the rules for the transformation of Amstel3? How can these be transparently conveyed, without making the process overly complex?

A Resilient and Sustainable Organisational Model

Another issue arises as the economic crisis is now considered to be over in Amsterdam. Investments are flowing to the city and the need for housing is high. Whilst the city council's growing temptation to take back the lead and start making big plans again is understandable, the creation of resilient cities calls for many shoulders to carry such schemes. It takes enormous effort to activate stakeholders who are used to being taken care of by the government, and to break through their often docile attitude. Community-based and real-time urban transformation of the kind ZO!City is pursuing is not a crisis solution, but a resilient and sustainable organisational model that reflects the rapid changes to which our cities are subject.

Scaling the Hyperlocal

As the TransformCity® dashboard continues to be tested in real-world situations, the platform is now being requested by other cities too. Digital tools are easily scalable and it is tempting to believe they can solve similar challenges everywhere. However, the local – spatial, cultural, institutional – context varies, depending on the city or neighbourhood concerned, and can have a significant impact on the success of the methods and tools used. Who needs to adapt to whom? A digital tool carries the intrinsic values of the people and contexts that created it. Other cities can learn and benefit from this, but ideally also make their own impact on the tool to make it genuinely customised and hyperlocal again.

TransformCity is currently setting up an extended pilot with five international cities to research what the different contexts need and how our methods and tools need to adapt to them. The initiative aims to deepen knowledge and experience exchange between cities, stakeholders and tools. Technology can be a facilitating, rather than a demanding, force for our cities, but we need to keep each other sharp. ⌂

Imagined Community and Networked Hyperlocal Publics

What is the place of both immediate and mediated information in forming publics and sustaining communities? And what can past communication practices teach us in our digitally hyperconnected age? With reference to the work of philosophers, sociologists and theorists including Hannah Arendt, Jürgen Habermas, Keith Hampton and Barry Wellman, cultural researcher **John Bingham-Hall** reflects on the nature of place, and highlights the phatic properties of online platforms such as Southeast London's Brockley Central blog that seek to reinforce local identity.

Brock

8w

e this

#streetart #brockley

Mural,
Brockley,
Southeast London,
2016

Instagram of a mural near the station in the Southeast London neighbourhood of Brockley showing its postcode district SE4. Urban space is and always has been performed as place through multiple layers of mediation: the postcode is a virtual boundary, represented as street art, documented in social media.

Why should we care about hyperlocal media? Because they will reinvent local democracy, connect citizens directly to one another in networks of cooperation and deliberation, produce data on the sentiments and opinions of constituents for their political representatives? Perhaps, though to attribute these utopian ideals to technology is to deny due credit to the physical labour still invested in the building of effective local publics. Communication technologies, for many designers, are imagined as instrumental: we should care about them because they help people do things.

Whether from the industry 'smart city' perspective or the more activist (though increasingly industry co-opted) 'smart citizen' framework, design thinking is focused on technology's ability to do things in new ways – its instrumental value for civic participation, citizen-created data, bottom-up planning and so on. Design is inherently future focused, encoding assumptions about what communication should be for, assuming that new ways of doing things will result in the disruption of pre-existing ways of sharing information.

Some new platforms have indeed impacted positively on the workings of localised political action. But this goal-oriented mode of technological innovation belies the lived reality of narratives and emotional affect through which people have always imagined their relationship with the spaces they inhabit and the publics they cohabit them with. What we call communication technologies now – whether

the hardware of devices, the software of platforms or the infrastructure of the Internet – are of course not the first technologies to encode, store and transmit information. But the particular technologie of the 21st century seem, as they are perceived to take us further from nature, to have amplified this instrumental mindset.

The Medium is the Message

For political philosopher Hannah Arendt, in 1958, publishing, or 'making public' through communication, was a way of creating a shared reality out of 'uncertain, shadowy' subjectivity.[1] In *Media, Modernity and Technology* (2006), sociologis David Morley foregrounds the 'phatic' role of communication – the polite greeting that has no instrumental value, but establishes public civility, for example.[2]

This process should not always be put to work. Communicative acts, from writing a letter to sending a tweet, have always had deeply symbolic qualities, the affect of which can supersede their content. Whether there can be phatic qualities to the masses of communication that now takes place solely between computers remains to be seen, but any transaction between humans, even if mediated, must be recognised as partially symbolic.

So to return to the question of why we should care about hyperlocal: it is because, to quote Arendt again, 'the presence of others who see what we see and hear what we hear assures us of the reality of the

Total Number of CONE and Country Code Domains by City, January 1999

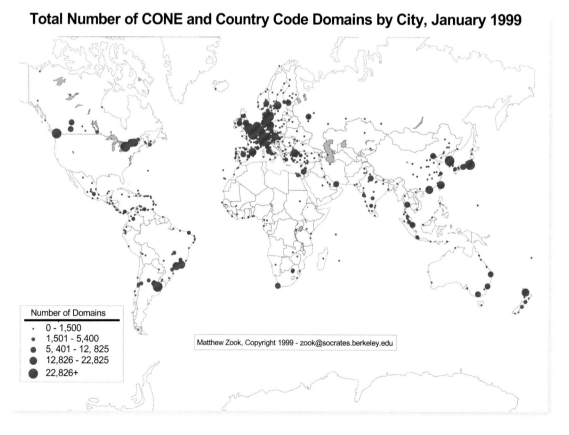

Matthew Zook, Copyright 1999 - zook@socrates.berkeley.edu

Number of Domains
- 0 - 1,500
- 1,501 - 5,400
- 5, 401 - 12, 825
- 12,826 - 22,825
- 22,826+

Map of global domain registrations by city, January 1999

Communication technology does not transcend space, but is shaped by patterns of urban concentration and inequality.

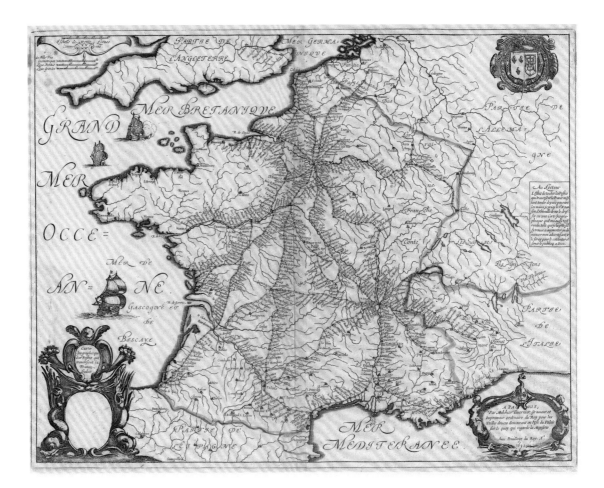

icolas Sanson's
ap of the national
ostal system in
rance,
632

he development
f networks of
ommunication in Europe
 the 17th century aided
he emergence of the
naginary of the nation as
socio-spatial unit.

world and ourselves'.[3] Understood as the adoption
of communication technologies for the circulation
of texts in and about neighbourhoods, hyperlocal
media is a setting to witness and experience the
meaningfulness of place alongside others doing the
same. Place is not just an inherent feature of space;
t is performed through the way spaces, and the
people and artefacts wrapped up in them, become
shared concerns, get discussed, become chronicled in
censuses and names, documented in watercolour or
on Instagram.

These acts of communication are rarely, on the
surface of it, useful. They are the public chatter given
value by Morley rather than the rational discourse
longed for by sociologist and philosopher Jürgen
Habermas in his classic analysis of the public sphere
published in 1962.[4] Their value is not in content, but
in the pathways they open up between people and
the subtle perceptual reinforcement of the coherence
of local identity. We will return to this after asking
another question: Why '4D' hyperlocal?

Historical Time as the Fourth Dimension
In the 1990s, Internet theory foregrounded the two-
dimensional affordances of this new technology:
flattening bodies, erasing physical and spatial
inequalities, becoming a value-free plane onto which
constructed identities could be projected. This new
aspatial world seemed an escape from the violence of

cities in the late 20th century, to the extent that one
commentator gleefully proclaimed: 'the solvent of
digital information decomposes traditional building
types.'[5]

In fact, the first time information could be
transmitted across space faster than it could be
carried by man or beast was with the invention of
the semaphore in 1792, which carried informational
codes at the speed of light (plus a little time for
operating the signals), allowing 'symbols to move
independently of geography' and producing what
felt then like a decoupling of ethereal media and the
contingency of the 'real' world.[6] Communication,
though, may traverse, but it does not transcend space.
It is always reliant on infrastructures, the issues
that living together generates, local knowledge and
language, even geology. The acknowledgement of
this in the early 21st century led to a concern for the
way geography shaped communication, moving the
discourse into three dimensions. In 2008, geographer
Matthew Zook showed at a global scale the uneven
geographies of the production of the Web's content.[7]
Around the turn of the 21st century, sociologists
Keith Hampton and Barry Wellman showed that
the introduction of the Internet into a previously
unwired suburb could intensify both local and global
awareness,[8] leading Wellman to propose the term
'glocalism'.[9]

But digital information is just another form of writing. According to foundational media theorist Marshall McLuhan in 1967, 'the goose quill' [early communication technology] … gave architecture and towns'.[10] Even writing was not the first way in which information was freed from the limitations of bodies together in space. John Durham Peters, in his 2015 history of 'elemental media', traces the writing of culture back to prelinguistic man: grave markings and cave paintings were a way of encoding and projecting memory through time.[11] Processing, storing and transmitting information, he argues, is the essence of the human, and media are the machines that do this work.

Time, of course, is the fourth dimension. But the historical is a timescale missing from our conception of the use of new communication technologies in cities. Are they really so new, so 'disruptive' (to use the popular tech-industry terminology)? Overemphasising continuity can be unhelpful – to imagine social media as unproblematically analogous to the Greek agora[12] is to hide so many communicative inequalities and distinct protocols it encodes (even if history has hidden the inequalities of the overly idealised agora itself). But a historical view of the way we communicate in cities is important. Futurology is all too easily co-opted as a sales pitch: 'I've seen the future, and my product will take you there.' As Laura Vaughan, Professor of Urban Form at the Bartlett School of Architecture, University College London (UCL), has argued, we will understand the future of cities by looking at their past.[13] The same is true of urban communication, and the technologies that facilitate it.

A Historically Grounded Open-Source City

So what do we learn from past communication practices in the city? Habermas linked the emergenc of a national social consciousness with the growth of postal systems, carried on horse overland and by trading ships from the Americas and Far East. The burgeoning trade in newspapers, supported by these expanding communication networks (after all, 17th-century trading ships carrying printed words across the seas were the transoceanic optical cables of their day), was bolstering a new 'reading public' of individuals in virtual, imagined communion with fellow readers of current affairs. Benedict Anderson describes the reading of newspapers as a daily 'ceremony' through which national societies are imagined through imagined commonality with unknown others.[14] Networks of communication have the processing power to transform geographica space into social place, through the circulation of shared texts, language and issues that hold discrete individuals together as the continuous form we call society.

So while 17th-century coffee houses are idealised as the sites of critical, unmediated political debate, in contrast to today's rooms of glowing screens, they actually relied on these flows of mediated information. Habermas foregrounds the rational and democratic nature of these gatherings, but they reveal something else: a timeless interflow between mediated and immediate. The public discourse that took place here was based on a shared focus on something external – the framing of issues as causes for public concern. No doubt it was also a pretext for togetherness, gossip, drinking, business deals: side effects of the public sphere that cannot be seen within the content of media.

Unknown artist, Interior of a London Coffee House, c 1695

Printed news traded across Europe provided the basis for debate – the line between the 'virtual' space of communication and the 'real' space of physical encounter is always blurred.

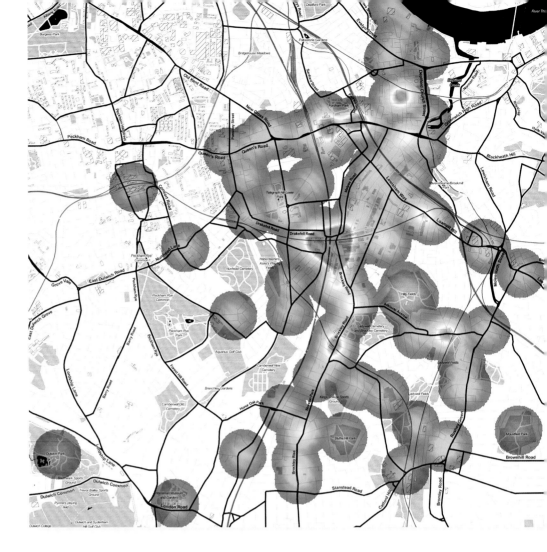

John Bingham-Hall, Heatmap of locations that are the topics of posts on the Brockley Central hyperlocal blog over two years, Space Syntax Laboratory, Bartlett School of Architecture, University College London (UCL), 2013-15

As postal networks helped to create a national territory, the distribution of these locations shapes the perception of hyperlocal place, but in uneven ways that are linked to spatial accessibility.

Even in the revered Roman forum, on the basis of which so many urban designers have tried to create public spaces for community encounter, conversation was based on affairs of the city that were documented and distributed by the gazette of the Senate. Media store, frame and transmit ideas giving common ground for face-to-face talk. We gather around screens, discuss books. All but the most intimate human contact is triangulated via an external reference point on a network of information flows much larger than our immediate experience.

Geographies and Ecologies of Hyperlocal Media

What does all this mean for hyperlocal media? The Southeast London neighbourhood of Brockley was an early adopter of hyperlocal media in the form of the Brockley Central blog, which was established in 2007.[15] Traces of all these enduring characteristics of media can be seen in the way Brockley's residents relate to the blog, to one another, and to the space in which they live.

Many of the blog's readers feel involved in local life simply by being informed, valuing the abstract sense of connection this offers over the actual ability to communicate with neighbours. This is borne out in the network of Twitter relationships in Brockley, which can be mapped by tracing the network of connections between Brockley Central's followers.[16] Highly connected profiles like Brockley Central and other blogs, local businesses, councillors, and a few vocal self-appointed spokespeople, produce a local public sphere of opinion on behalf of an audience of onlookers with few of their own interconnections. This is not a public sphere of direct encounter between people, but of triangulation via well-known local people and issues.

Readers interviewed speak about an abstract 'we' and 'us', representing an imaginary of social cohesion belonging to a specific space, without needing or indeed wanting to actually know of whom it consists. This assuredness of belonging to a common world is a phatic property of the local public sphere: what matters is not what is being discussed, but the fact that 'we' are reading it and have an opinion. The space of that common world is strongly shaped, in the minds of its readers, by the distribution of locations the blog covers. Brockley as a place becomes in some sense created unevenly. It is a public realm strongly present along the main road, which is also the location of the most connected businesses on Twitter, and less so in surrounding residential areas. As Matthew Zook showed globally, centralised locations are also more effective at producing the public sphere on a hyperlocal scale.

Sometimes residents do come into contact, though, in cafes, at events or by being retweeted by a local business. The abstract is kept alive by materialising as something physical from time to time, but the smoothness of these physical encounters relies on the abstract realm. Talk with strangers and acquaintances is based on the external focus on local issues or goings on. Brockley Central ensures a common awareness of and interest in these issues. Though it is a specific, largely middle-class public that reads the blog, it is no coincidence that it is the same public that goes to the cafes, shops, restaurants and local events it recommends. There is a feedback loop between mediated and immediate public life.

The Tyranny of Community

Anonymity and impersonality endure, though. They have always been a feature of cities, since the idle gossiping and political posturing of the Roman forum, and earlier. They enable urban society to be progressive and liberal as opposed to what sociologist Richard Sennett has called the 'tyranny' of the community.[17] Shared concern for issues form publics[18] – loose, conflictual, constantly changing social constellations in specific but overlapping spaces – rather than communities, which are spatially bounded, static and in consensus. The hyperlocal public is a subset of the wider public sphere, supported by the circulation of local stories through a multiplex network of blogs, Twitter, face-to-face chat, leaflets, posters on trees and so on. The value of this network is not necessarily what it can do. Instead its symbolic value and its physical layout gives its hyperlocal public, in the words of media scholar Sandra Ball-Rokeach, the 'ability to "imagine" an area as a community' through 'stories about "us" in this geographical space'.[19] ⌀

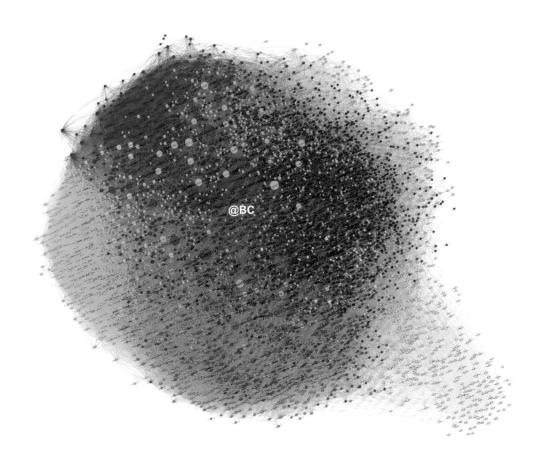

John Bingham-Hall and Stephen Law, Network map of Brockley Central Twitter followers, Space Syntax Laboratory, Bartlett School of Architecture, University College London (UCL), 2014

Each profile is represented by a dot sized according to its number of followers and in colour groups of densely connected profiles. The local Twitter-sphere is focused around well-connected businesses and public figures, with individual residents as onlookers mostly disconnected from one another.

Legend
Total degree

7351
1

PeckhamPlatform

TheAlbanySE8   DeptfordProject
                DeptfordLounge
theparticular   thebigredpizza
No178 NewCross NewCrossHouse
                theroyalalbert

BrockleyMarket

The Gantry The Orchard
            GentlyE

BrockleysRock

Save Ivy House
DishSE15   ElsKitchenLadyw

jamcircus
ArloMoe
BrocJackTheatre

hopscotchbar
dondetapas

catfordtavern

HornimanMuseum

John Bingham-
Hall, Locations
of businesses in
Brockley Central's
Twitter network, Space
Syntax Laboratory,
Bartlett School
of Architecture,
University College
London (UCL),
2014

Size indicates the number
of followers in the network,
with colours drawn from
the network map. The most
connected profiles are located
along the main road, and
businesses that are linked
spatially are more likely to
follow one another.

Notes

1. Hannah Arendt, 'The Public Realm: The Common', in Mark Lilla and Nathan Glazer (eds), *The Public Face of Architecture*, The Free Press (London and New York), 1987, p 7.

2. David Morley, *Media, Modernity and Technology: The Geography of the New*, Routledge (Abingdon), 2007.

3. Arendt, *op cit*, pp 5–6.

4. Jürgen Habermas, *The Structural Transformation of the Public Sphere: An Inquiry Into a Category of Bourgeois Society*, MIT Press (Cambridge, MA), 1991.

5. William J Mitchell, *City of Bits: Space, Place, and the Infobahn*, MIT Press (Cambridge, MA and London), 1996, p 47.

6. James W Carey, 'Time, Space, and the Telegraph', in David J Crowley and Paul Heyer (eds), *Communication History: Technology, Culture, Society*, Pearson Allyn & Bacon (Boston, MA), 2007, pp 125–31.

7. Matthew Zook, *The Geography of the Internet*, Blackwell (Oxford), 2005.

8. Keith Hampton and Barry Wellman, 'Neighboring in Netville: How the Internet Supports Community and Social Capital in a Wired Suburb', *City & Community*, 2 (4), 2003, pp 277–311.

9. Barry Wellman, 'Physical Place and Cyberplace: The Rise of Personalized Networking', *International Journal of Urban and Regional Research*, 25 (2), 2001, p 236.

10. Marshall McLuhan and Quentin Fiore, *The Medium Is the Massage: An Inventory of Effects*, Penguin (London), 1967, p 48.

11. John Durham Peters, *The Marvelous Clouds: Toward a Philosophy of Elemental Media*, University of Chicago Press (Chicago, IL), 2015.

12. As in Mitchell, *op cit*, p 8.

13. Laura S Vaughan, 'Is the Future of Cities the Same as Their Past?', in Ben Campkin and Rebecca Ross (eds), *Urban Pamphleteer #1: Future and Smart Cities*, 1, 26 April 2013, pp 20–22.

14. Benedict Anderson, *Imagined Communities: Reflections on the Origin and Spread of Nationalism*, Verso (London and New York), 1983.

15. And which the author has been researching since 2015 in his ongoing PhD research at the Bartlett School of Architecture, University College London (UCL), funded in full by the UK Engineering & Physical Sciences Research Council: www.bartlett.ucl. ac.uk/space-syntax/people/mphil-phd-students/john-bingham-hall.

16. John Bingham-Hall and Stephen Law, 'Connected or Informed?: Local Twitter Networking in a London Neighbourhood', *Big Data & Society*, 2 (2), 1 July 2015.

17. Richard Sennett, *The Fall of Public Man*, Penguin (London), 2002, p 297.

18. John Law, Karel Williams and Johal Sukhdev, 'From Publics to Congregations', *CRESC Working Papers*, Centre for Research on Socio-Cultural Change (Manchester and Milton Keynes), 2014.

19. Yong-Chan Kim and Sandra J Ball-Rokeach, 'Civic Engagement From a Communication Infrastructure Perspective', *Communication Theory*, 16 (2), 2006, p 178.

Laura Kurgan

Conflict Urbanism, Aleppo Mapping Urban Damage

Center for Spatial Research, Conflict Urbanism:
Aleppo – informal settlements and urban damage,

Graduate School of Architecture, Planning and
Preservation (GSAPP),

Columbia University,

New York,

2015

The map depicts patterns of documented urban damage in Aleppo, Syria. Damaged sites that have been identified by the United Nations Institute for Training and Research (UNITAR) Operational Satellite Operations Programme (UNOSAT) as of 1 May 2015 (the orange dots) are primarily located in the northern, eastern and southeastern portions of the city; 42 per cent of these damaged sites fall within 'informally' developed areas (outlined in white).

One of the oldest continuously inhabited cities on the planet, Aleppo now lies in tatters. This devastation of a designated World Heritage Site is a poignant example of the human and cultural cost of armed conflict – in this case the Syrian Civil War. A project run by the Center for Spatial Research at the Graduate School of Architecture, Planning and Preservation of New York's Columbia University is analysing satellite imagery and reports from the ground to assess the damage and casualties caused there by barrel bombs. Associate Professor **Laura Kurgan** describes the initiative and its sometimes puzzling findings.

More than five years after the start of the civil war in Syria, its largest city, Aleppo, is still under siege. Hundreds of thousands of Syrians have been killed or injured, and an estimated nine million people have been displaced. Aleppo has suffered extensive physical damage – to its symbolic centre, the Citadel; to its surrounding heritage sites, which mark ancient empires, diverse religions, and multiple cultures and trade routes; and to its eastern and southern neighbourhoods. The destruction of the city's cultural and urban history, as well as its cultural memory and identity, appears to be an intentional result of military operations, and not merely a byproduct of them.

In *The Destruction of Memory: Architecture at War* (2006),[1] Robert Bevan understands the destruction of cities in wartime in terms of attacks not simply on buildings and people, but on memory. Dresden and Baghdad typify this phenomenon. The annihilation of culture is certainly visible in the civil war in Aleppo, a UNESCO World Heritage site, as well. But there are other object lessons here too. For while war demolishes, it also reshapes a city, and, however difficult it is to imagine rebuilding in the midst of a war, Aleppo is being restructured and will be rebuilt. To Bevan's thesis that memory is destroyed by war, it is necessary to add that memories are also created during war, and urban rebuilding in the aftermath is faced with either addressing or erasing these.

For example, in the memorial at the World Trade Center in New York, the destruction wrought there on 11 September 2001 is itself commemorated with a simulation of the rebuilding of the foundation holes of the two towers, the names of the dead engraved into the surrounding walls. The tower is built anew on a different site, so as not to erase the scene of destruction. Compare this with the historical district of Warsaw in Poland, where the city centre, bombed by the German air force in 1939 and then obliterated by the army in 1944, was reconstructed after the war to replicate as exactly as possible its prewar appearance.

The Center for Spatial Research at the Graduate School of Architecture, Planning and Preservation (GSAPP), Columbia University, New York, is currently undertaking an investigative project to try to understand the past, present, as well as a future Aleppo. As part of the research, an interactive map is now publicly available with layers of high-resolution satellite images showing the city from 2012 to the present. Using the logic of a typical geographic information system (GIS) map, the Conflict Urbanism, Aleppo project overlaps these layers, accruing evidence of destruction. But what type of model do the layers build?

GIS layers are often treated as objective fact, but data is not neutral – it is always designed and packaged, demanding interrogation. What are the sources of the data? What do they intend to document? What are the measures of conflict? What kinds of evidence can high-resolution satellite views afford us? Do records of urban damage complement or complicate records of human casualties?

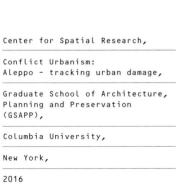

Center for Spatial Research,

Conflict Urbanism:
Aleppo - tracking urban damage,

Graduate School of Architecture,
Planning and Preservation
(GSAPP),

Columbia University,

New York,

2016

The graph compares the number of documented deaths recorded by the Violations Documentation Center in Aleppo Province and the number of damaged buildings documented by UNOSAT in and around Aleppo. It reveals that the destruction of buildings in the city has continued even while the number of deaths has apparently declined.

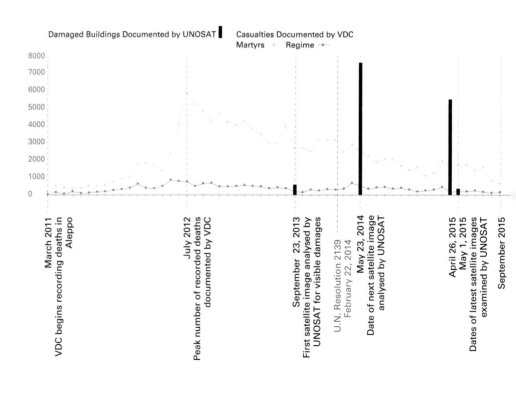

al-'Aqabeh, 1 May 2012

al-'Aqabeh, 3 September 2015

Center for Spatial Research,
Conflict Urbanism: Aleppo – high-
resolution satellite images of
three Aleppo neighbourhoods on
1 May 2012 and 3 September 2015,

Graduate School of Architecture,
Planning and Preservation (GSAPP),

Columbia University,

New York,

2015

The three pairs of satellite images show damaged buildings in the central neighbourhood of al-'Aqabeh, flattened industrial buildings in Tal az-Zarazir, and damaged residential buildings in Karm aj-Jabal. Circles drawn by Human Rights Watch have been superimposed onto the high-resolution images to mark damaged sites, many of which were caused by barrel bombs. These improvised unguided aerial missiles leave a particular imprint on the city, carving out larger zones of impact with more irregular edges than other types of aerial missiles.

Understanding War's Erasure of Culture

The concept of 'urban vandalism', which has served as a motivating rationale and theoretical framework for the Center's Aleppo project, stems from Polish-Jewish lawyer Raphael Lemkin, who coined the term 'genocide' during the Second World War, and campaigned tirelessly for the Convention on the Prevention and Punishment of the Crime of Genocide, adopted by the UN General Assembly in 1948 and entered into force in 1951 after ratification by 20 states. Back in 1933, Lemkin had described what he called 'offences against the law of nations' through two interlinked concepts: 'barbarity' and 'vandalism'. Barbarity became the core of the notion of genocide, primarily as 'acts of extermination' targeting 'ethnic, religious or social collectivities', while vandalism was the 'systematic and organized destruction of the art and cultural heritage in which the unique genius and achievement of a collectivity are revealed in fields of science, arts and literature'.[2]

Vandalism did not make it into the Genocide convention, but is reflected in the 1954 Hague Convention for the Protection of Cultural Property in the Event of Armed Conflict (effective in 1956). Although international criminal law has since incorporated 'the destruction of cultural heritage' into the understanding of genocide – the UN Tribunal for ex-Yugoslavia noted that 'where there is physical or biological destruction there are often simultaneous attacks on the cultural and religious property and symbols of the targeted group as well, attacks which may legitimately be considered as evidence of an intent to physically destroy the group' – it remains difficult to try this erasure of culture in a court of law.[3]

Analyses of Time-Based Satellite Imagery and On-Ground Reporting

Two satellite images of Aleppo, from 1 May 2012 (from the DigitalGlobe constellation of satellites) and 3 September 2015 (from Pleiades), can be analysed in relation to an interpretive dataset created by international non-governmental organisation Human Rights Watch.[4] Assessing the use of barrel bombs in the city after a United Nations resolution forbade the use of such weapons, Human Rights Watch annotated these satellite images, circling damaged sites. These improvised unguided aerial missiles leave a particular imprint on the city, carving out larger zones of impact with more irregular edges than other types of aerial missiles. Human Rights Watch uses this kind of imagery analysis to record potential war crimes and violations of UN resolutions (for future use in courts of law) and to raise public awareness of the violence. The 'before' and 'after' images zoom in on three neighbourhoods, looking at destroyed homes in Sheikh Sa'eed, a row of damaged structures in al-'Aqabeh, and flattened industrial buildings in Tal az-Zarazir.

While Human Rights Watch focuses on the precise shape of the impact sites and the weapons used, it is also important to look at what surrounds the circles – the areas contiguous to the damaged sites – in order to ask questions on an urban scale. Several lines of inquiry are emerging: What are the relationships between the informal settlements that appeared in Aleppo before the war and the patterns of bombing inflicted by the Damascus regime? Has the destruction of the built environment continued despite the forced migration from the city of Aleppo residents? What information about the conflict is revealed by looking specifically at urban damage visible from satellite images?

The Violations Documentation Center (VDC), a Syria-based network of opposition activists, has focused on deaths, injuries, detentions and disappearances of individuals, recording the identities of the victims, and the causes and locations of these violations. Separate records are kept for 'martyrs' (both civilians and members of rebel groups are labelled such) and for 'regime fatalities' (members of the Syrian Army or other armed forces of the Damascus regime).[5] Among the multiple datasets on casualties, the VDC dataset contains the most information, but it can in no way be considered complete. As Megan Price, Jeff Klingner and Patrick Ball suggest in their 'Preliminary Statistical Analysis of Documentation of Killings in the Syrian Arab Republic' (2013),[6] this is typical in relation to human rights, for many reasons, from difficulty of collection to the ways in which it is reported. The uncertainty this creates – along with questions regarding the methods and aims of the data collection – makes this important dataset almost unusable at the neighbourhood level.

Since 2012, the VDC has recorded a decline in the number of documented deaths. However, records of damaged buildings from the United Nations Operational Satellite Applications Programme (UNOSAT) complicate this narrative. UNOSAT also examines high-resolution satellite imagery to identify and record visible damage. Since 2013, it has continued to locate and document large numbers of damaged buildings in Aleppo.[7] Plotting these alongside the VDC data reveals that the destruction of buildings has continued even while the number of deaths has apparently declined.

Though the conflation of these two types of data – satellite imagery analysis by UNOSAT and on-ground reporting by the VDC – might be expected to give a comprehensive picture of the conflict in Aleppo, it instead opens up more questions. Why, for instance, has there been a decline in the number of recorded deaths and an increase in the number of damaged buildings? This is an important

Karma aj-Jabal, 1 May 2012

Karma aj-Jabal, 3 September 2015

The critical perspectives that emerge from these analyses of time-based satellite imagery alongside other documentation of the Aleppo conflict urge a reframing of existing narratives of the violence of war.

Tal az-Zarazir, 1 May 2012

Tal az-Zarazir, 3 September 2015

question because, if it is true, it indicates that there has not been a decline in violence. The decline in deaths, even as aerial bombardment continued, could be the result of the mass migration of Syrian civilians, or, just as plausibly, caused by the VDC having fewer volunteers on the ground to record casualties.

Reframing Existing Narratives

The critical perspectives that emerge from these analyses of time-based satellite imagery alongside other documentation of the Aleppo conflict urge a reframing of existing narratives of the violence of war. They also help in understanding urban damage itself as a crucial dimension of contemporary conflict that requires much further work. Initiatives by the Center for Spatial Research that advance its focus on Aleppo are therefore ongoing – the project's website, for example, hosts an interactive mapping platform that includes a publicly browsable, neighbourhood-level map of Aleppo – and involve the curating of data of urban destruction in such a way that memory is preserved, rather than destroyed. ⚿

Notes
1. Robert Bevan, *The Destruction of Memory: Architecture at War*, Reaktion (London), 2006.
2. Donald Bloxham and A Dirk Moses, *The Oxford Handbook of Genocide Studies*, Oxford University Press (Oxford and New York), 2010, pp 31–2.
3. André Klip and Göran Sluiter (eds), *Annotated Leading Cases of International Criminal Tribunals*, Intersentia (Antwerp), 1999, p 732.
4. Human Rights Watch Satellite Imagery Analysis Team, 'Impact Sites', 22 February 2014 to 3 September 2015, cited in Kenneth Roth, 'To Stem the Flow of Syrian Refugees, Stop the Barrel Bombs', Human Rights Watch, 23 September 2015: www. hrw.org/news/2015/09/23/stem-flow-syrian-refugees-stop-barrel-bombs.
5. Violations Documentation Center Records for Aleppo Province, March 2011 to September 2015: http://www.vdc-sy.info/index.php/en/.
6. Megan Price, Jeff Klingner and Patrick Ball, 'Preliminary Statistical Analysis of Documentation of Killings in the Syrian Arab Republic', Benetech Human Rights Program, United Nations Office of the High Commissioner for Human Rights (OHCHR). 2013: http://www.ohchr.org/Documents/Countries/SY/PreliminaryStatAnalysisKillingsInSyria.pdf.
7. UNOSAT, 'Damage Assessment of Aleppo, Aleppo Governorate, Syria', 23 September 2013 to 1 May 2015: www.unitar.org/unosat/node/44/2238?utm_source=unosat-unitar&utm_medium=rss&utm_campaign=maps.

Raffaele Pe

Suburban Resonance in Segrate, Milan

Degraded buildings in Milan Segrate, 2014

The highly infrastructural district of Milan is being reconstituted with numerous newly developed dwellings facing Milan's Parco Sud. Their presence and their appearance do not seem to enrich the local identity, conveying a sense of bewilderment.

The Language of Locative Media in Defining Urban Sensitivity

Interactive platforms are opening up the possibility of an aural approach to spatial design. **Raffaele Pe**, a lecturer in the Department of Architecture and Urban Studies at the Politecnico di Milano,

Parco Agricolo Sud,
Milan,
2014

The metropolitan park surrounds part of the city, penetrating the urban fringes and creating a set of undetermined spaces where it is not possible to develop agriculture because of the dimension of the plots. Here, a water feature in front of small unproductive fields is transformed into a park facing high-rise dwellings at the border of the city.

here examines the advantages of a locative media approach to architecture, urban and landscape design, with specific reference to the urban-rural Milanese suburb of Segrate, the focus of an investigative project led with his department.

When exploited for urban design purposes, locative media – that is, digital media applied to real places – allow the construction of interactive ambiences by giving city users the opportunity to collaborate with designers to produce a shared vision of the future development of the city. While establishing multiple links between material and immaterial parts of our urban environment through predefined interfaces, this contribution enhances the understanding of digital design as the metalanguage of a process in which all the harvested data relate to each other through actions of site-specific sonification for inventive spatial configuration. The common, narrow consideration of the hyperlocal as a set of data that emerges from the survey of specific hyperlocal websites needs to be re-evaluated in favour of the idea of topographic scripting as a resonating instrument to orientate and determine what can be termed the 'musical' spatial behaviour of urban inhabitants.

The application of locative digital technologies to architecture and urban planning constitutes a design asset that enables a process of spatial configuration to be supported while at the same time framing site-specific urban events. As suggested by media and communications theorist Caroline Bassett, locative media intercept the user's interests with emerging sites in our territories.[1] The continuous flow of hyperlocal data constitutes a set of relevant information for the design process if we interpret the project as a threshold between a tempered environment and users' trajectories. The body of space as a whole becomes available for inhabitation, mutating the way we usually perceive suburban neglected sites. When the language used is able to attract people, locative devices such as GPS trackers and geo-referenced social networks awake cooperation and engagement, building a sense of belonging to a place in its inhabitants.

Therefore the question is, which modes of expression are more appropriate to explore the intangible and yet sensorial potential of locative media for urban reform? Spatial mapping through digital media is a means to enhance urban performance within the environment of our metropolis, especially across those communities who populate areas that are neglected and debased. The assessment of neglected areas often presents issues of orientation and localisation with regards to the disclosure of the intrinsic qualities of such seemingly inaccessible urban enclaves.

The political boundaries given to Segrate, an eastern suburban district of Milan, for example, reflect a limited understanding of the current topographic role this location is playing in the development of the metropolitan system. For, while the authorities address Segrate as an enclosed urban entity, detached from the surrounding built environment, the current sprawl of buildings and infrastructures highlights a more transient exchange happening between the core of the old village and the unproductive protected rural landscape of Milan's Parco Agricolo Sud. Established in 1990 to protect the natural and historical assets of the Po Valley, and covering 47,000 hectares (116,000 acres), Parco Sud is one of Milan's major green and water features that encircles the city towards the east, south and west.

Beneath the Tangenziale motorway, Milan, 2014

A park with landscape elements is hidden underneath Milan's Tangenziale motorway.

Segrate is a paradigm of many of our fast-developing modern cities in which fragmented urban regions often constitute an architectural modulation of the gap between metropolitan and rural ecosystems. As such, it has been the subject of a locative media architecture and design project developed in collaboration with the Politecnico di Milano's Department of Architecture and Urban Studies, with the contribution of Alessandro Musetta and Stefano Bovio. When looking at the configuration of this region more closely we realise that the term 'suburban' cannot always be used as synonymous with 'peripheral'. As a territory, Milan Segrate stands in the middle of a highly accessible urban sector – featuring the presence of Linate airport and geographically contiguous to the city centre and the main hubs of the urban network – yet it is easy to describe as suburban. The imposing presence of Parco Sud does not seem to produce positive effects

Locative media enhance our surveying capacity. They provide two ways of managing spatial transformation: on one hand they strengthen our analytical capabilities in a statistical and

on the realisation of a more liveable and integrated environment within such a composite landscape.

The construction of a map that is able to picture objectively the characteristics of a suburban context for its future development requires the definition of a set of values that encompasses its fleeting and unstable character while delineating the premises for its activation and transformation. Moreover the map should offer the possibility of working both on a practical level for the coordination of people's spatial movements and through an abstract perspective, in order to consider the inhabitants' learning processes concerning the city as part of a comprehensive urban design methodology.

Locative media enhance our surveying capacity. They provide two ways of managing spatial transformation: on one hand they strengthen our analytical capabilities in a statistical and essentially objective way; on the other hand they foster our inventiveness in evaluating available assets for the future conversion of places. Sensors, GPS trackers and radio-frequency identification (RFID) devices, exploited as tools

Infrastructures and spontaneous vegetation, Milan, 2014

Wild vegetation on buildings and around urban voids increases a sense of decadence while enhancing environmental biodiversity.

essentially objective way; on the other hand they foster our inventiveness in evaluating available assets for the future conversion of places.

for environmental monitoring, structure a correspondence between the biographies of places and the agenda of their users, interweaving history and geography. Digital technologies for landscape framing and design can be envisaged as an 'art object'[2] through which data processing becomes an engine for spatial imagination and integration.

The Formulation of an Aural Language

Communication technologies ease navigation of our cities, augmenting our perceptive capacities in space and time. As Marshall McLuhan would have said, they have transformed our environment into a collaborative aural laboratory.[3] The space of modern electronic technologies is the space of the acoustic flow of information, where participation in knowledge is achieved through ephemeral waves that vibrate with variable rhythm and frequencies.

An urban context like that of Milan Segrate is endemically constituted by moving and unstable elements that are relevant as stationary references to orient our movements in its space. Also suburbs and sensitive urban sites display moving elements which, through their shifting conditions, help to shape the image of the city.[4] The image embodies the lineaments of the built environment while retaining the elusive traces of recurrent spatial behaviours.

Through locative media, architecture and urban design exploit more advanced forms of mapping to frame the unstable quality of this unfolding landscape. In this way urban design can then be addressed as a temporal art, in which objective elements and imagined components collaborate to express how the pace and the dynamics of our movements establish the deep reasons of the form of our habitat. The composition of a map through digital tools marks the passage from an acoustic insight to a musical language.

In an aural approach to spatial design, only a musical response can retain and transmit the meaning of our rationally conceived urban environment, even where rational forms are latent or weak. In artistic praxis, music could be interpreted as the discipline that presides over the spatial activation of a rhythm. According to composer Franco Donatoni, 'musical composition is an object that shares its destiny with most things that are manifested in the world, participating in the multiplicity of relationships that emerge in the universe'.[5] The musicianship embodied within a movement finds in space its appropriate pace allowing its most suitable unfolding: a sustainable configuration.

As medieval and then Renaissance culture remind us, music is our body's favourite tool to measure space, because of its ability to assign a tangible meaning to mathematical abstract proportions and calculations.[6] As Carolyn Abbate has written in her introduction to Vladimir Jankélévitch's *Music and the Ineffable*: 'Music is no cipher, […] Music has a power over our bodies and minds wildly disproportionate to its lack of obvious and concrete meaning, […] musical devices and processes are always bound to a human experience of time, to culture and the past.'[7] Sound as an unmistakable – scientific – measuring tool introduces us to the field of sound maps and audio-guides to outline a new geography for the senses.[8]

Urban maps that are produced through employing aural signals to build open learning frameworks on the external environment are neither nominal nor descriptive. They replace two-dimensional cartography with a generative prototype –

Raffaele Pe in collaboration with Politecnico di Milano, Department of Architecture and Urban Studies, Alessandro Musetta and Stefano Bovio, Milan Segrate locative media architecture and urban design project, 2015

The map of spatial criticalities at Milan Segrate is based on urban sensitivity indicators. The various areas of Segrate are thematised with different colours in relation to the degree of accessibility. Hyperlocal data outlines a diverse range of sensitivity levels in locations according to various indicators such as accessibility, availability of services and infrastructural pressure.

creenplays of complementary layers of urban data – which
onsiders the map as a performing tool for orientation,
ynchronised with the breath of the city. The employment of
nusic in this action provides experimental forms of mapping
hat allow the body to experience the sensorial condition of
he place in a new way.[9] Experimental maps communicate the
erforming essence of things directly to the senses, revealing
 more instinctive degree of spatial knowledge. Musical maps
xpress the inner and immaterial qualities of architecture, its
ransformational extent.

A Spatial Transformation for Milan Segrate

The construction in 2015 of the aural experimental map for
Milan Segrate is the fruit of a convoluted process of collaboration
between statistical data and destabilising glitches. This sound
map prototype as revealing art object intends to provide a
synthetic sensorial translation of the incidental condition of the
landscape in order to invite the reader to a subjective assessment
of the accessibility of the place.[10] The sound is an unambiguous
yet variable signal, whose meaning emerges confronting a
topographic contingency with an inventory of artistic assertions
that aim to delineate a specific spatial character. The collision

between statistics and artefacts promotes an abductive way of
creating knowledge across a wide community of city users.

The digital extent of the map implements its experimental
mode, transforming the device into a sound ambience, informed
by georeferenced real-time feeds. Architects and urban designers
here expand the pioneering work of Luciano Berio and Bruno
Maderna in their radio-drama *Ritratto di Città* (*Portrait of a
City*, 1954), a visionary documentary that describes a modern
city only mixing sound excerpts recorded on site with musical
material written specifically to express the sense of belonging to
the place.

A correspondence is established between places – assessed
according to their sensitivity – and depicting sounds. The concept
of urban sensitivity refers to the adaptability of a place due
to sociological, biological, environmental and technological
parameters.[11] The atypical quality of neglected places engages
with their openness to change. These sites are interpreted as
dynamic entities, incomplete systems, continually exchanging
with the other layers of the built environment – those that
constitute the landscape as a thick texture of heterogeneous
relationships.[12] The distribution of neglected spaces in Milan
Segrate presents several concentrations which constitute the

The rhythmically conceived
aural map proposes different
cadences according to
the topographic features
that emerged from urban
sensitivity maps. The territory
of Segrate is shown in grey,
with red spots of criticalities
and a superimposed
grid anticipating future
development of the district as
conceived by the embedded
masterplan.

premises for the renovation of the urban milieu within the historical and morphological framework of the region.

The degree of urban sensitivity in various areas of Milan Segrate expresses the urban–rural dichotomy as a singular dimension of the territory, where the two elements can strongly cooperate for the implementation of a feasible and coherent development of the local identity. The map outlines the resonance of these places, building a tempered system of sounds and signs according to the material accessibility to the place. All locations are inscribed within the spatial body of the city, inviting users to evaluate the meaning of each signal. In this way the resonance of what the European Spatial Planning Observation Network (ESPON) in its 2007 Guidelines has defined as 'urban sensitivity indicators' suggests the mitigation of the sense of bewilderment that some suburban regions can raise, avoiding the use of derogative definitions in regard to sites that are less gentrified or more peripheral or disrupted.[13]

If musical composition may seem the product of an artistic attitude, the art historian Erwin Panofsky reminds us that in films, as in any multimedia device, a bi-univocal bond is established across each integrated artefact so that a sound cannot be experienced without the image for which it was conceived, and vice versa.[14] Likewise a lighting design cannot be applied to a set other than the one for which it was originally devised. The bond of coexpressibility is an intrinsic condition of aural locative media. This concept introduces the possibility of exploiting unprecedented sensorial twists to implement the cognition and the interpretation of urban statistics, in order to reform neglected areas. Such a structure evokes a set of reactions in users' minds and bodies as they explore these areas through the device – an operation that translates a masterplan into a multimedia immanent site-specific project for the regeneration of an urban habitat.

The Milan Segrate aural map characterises urban sensitivity indicators with a tonal chromaticism. The map adopts a selection of available GIS data displayed in density graphs in order to define synthetic indicators of urban accessibility. The pairing and insertion of the indicators aim to translate the complex range of interactions that are established among all forces that generate the landscape as a dynamic entity into a navigation prototype. The issues that cause the state of abandonment of place are thematised, hence the tools needed for its reactivation are identified.

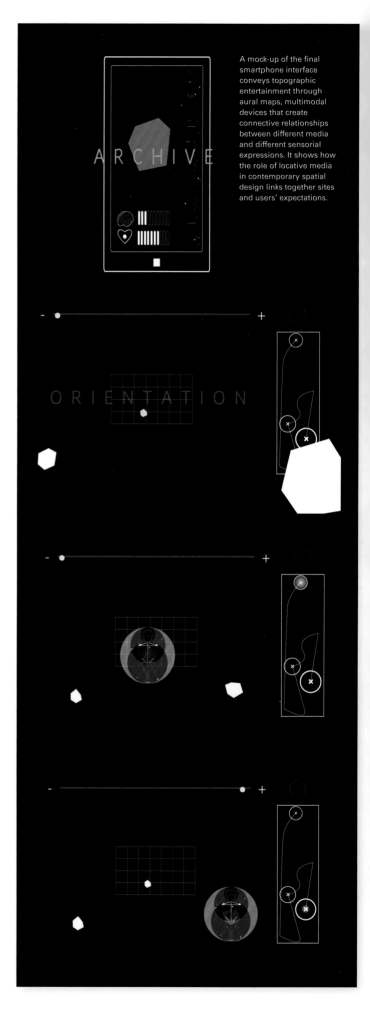

A mock-up of the final smartphone interface conveys topographic entertainment through aural maps, multimodal devices that create connective relationships between different media and different sensorial expressions. It shows how the role of locative media in contemporary spatial design links together sites and users' expectations.

The Milan Segrate aural map characterises urban sensitivity indicators with a tonal chromaticism.

Emerging routes: the use of hyperlocal aural maps along the masterplan's structures introduces a distortion in the configuration of the paths. The sonification of topographic data transforms a modular structure into a more flexible and twisted system.

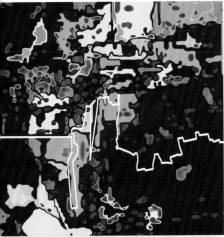

Emerging routes: with the Forlanini route the longest of all, cars are required to drive slowly towards the airport and then the countryside.

Emerging routes: rhythmical instability and spatial drifts correspond to a chromatic control of users' trajectories. Tones and speeds are the main parameters for the process of signification of place, imagining locative-media-driven urban design as a recreational practice.

Emerging routes: the node represents here the historical nucleus of Segrate providing a short route along which one can encounter the origins of this settlement.

Creating a Participatory Tool through Sonification

In general, the outcome of statistical urban analysis needs to be directly accountable by all users to create a participatory equipment for spatial orientation, however rarely ordinary infographics enhance any receptiveness in their users. The aural prototype implies an alphabet of different tonalities to characterise each indicator as a musical/visual entertainment that people can frame with their own language, linking the map to any commercial music streaming, podcast or video service.

This device becomes an essential tool for geographers, planners and architects, providing a metalanguage that enacts a communication network between Milan Segrate and users. Four different routes emerge from the Segrate prototype, offering users four different speeds of navigation. The musical narrative eases the exploration of the place, facilitating drifts through the landscape and inspiring imagination in the interpretation of the locations encountered.

Navigating the city should not be only a matter of functionality, but also one of curiosity and attraction – something playful and engaging. Sonification practices foster participation and involvement in this process in order to create custom paths to move within the city. Each emerging path is not just a sequence of play, stop, resume or rewind in a space–time dimension; instead, it facilitates the reordering of our urban archive through a flexible and modular procedure. The visual translation and the personalisation of places operated by processes of sonification is not a mere juxtaposition of acoustic events, but it is a composition with an information-centric approach based on georeferenced hyperlocal data. ⌂

Notes
1. Caroline Bassett, 'How Many Movements?', in Michael Bull and Les Beck (eds), *Auditory Culture Reader*, Berg (Oxford), 2003, pp 343–54.
2. See Hans-Georg Gadamer, 'The Relevance of the Beautiful', *The Relevance of the Beautiful and Other Essays*, ed Robert Bernasconi, trans Nicholas Walker, Cambridge University Press (Cambridge), 1986.
3. See Marshall McLuhan and Quentin Fiore, *The Medium is the Message: An Inventory of Effects*, Penguin (London), 1967.
4. Kevin Lynch, *The Image of the City*, MIT Press (Cambridge, MA), 1960, p 3.
5. Franco Donatoni, *Questo*, Adelphi (Milan), 1970, pp 62–3 (translation by Raffaele Pe).
6. See Diego Fratelli's explanation of the musical representation of the celestial orbits of the planets of our Solar System in Johannes Kepler's treaty *Harmonices Mundi* (1619), in Raffaele Pe, *Spazi Aurali: Architettura e Sound Design*, Postmedia Books (Milan), 2016, p 160.
7. Carolyn Abbate, 'Introduction', in Vladimir Jankélévitch, *Music and the Ineffable*, Princeton University Press (Princeton, NJ), 2003, pp xiii–xx.
8. Franco Farinelli, *Geografia*, Einaudi (Turin), 2003, p 201.
9. See Gilles Deleuze, Félix Guattari, *Rhizome*, Semiotext(e) (New York), 1983, p 25.
10. For a full experience of the Milan Segrate prototype, see www.soundofthings.org.
11. See ESPON, European Spatial Planning Observation Network Guidelines, 2007.
12. On the notion of landscape urbanism and urban ecology, see Charles Waldheim (ed), *The Landscape Urbanism Reader*, Princeton Architectural Press (Princeton, NJ), 2006.
13. See ESPON 2007, *op cit*.
14. See Erwin Panofsky, *Three Essays on Style*, ed Irving Lavin, MIT Press (Cambridge, MA), 1997.

Usman Haque

Umbrellium,

VoiceOver,

Horden,

County Durham,

2016

Different voices and sounds
created different patterns
and rhythms of colour that
bounced back and forth across
the VoiceOver mesh network
created.

VoiceOver

Citizen
Empowerment
Through Cultural
Infrastructure

A mesh-network was set up
with local residents, enabling
them to listen into the VoiceOver
network through a 'radio box'.

In the relentless drive for efficiency, our lives are increasingly dominated by decision-making algorithms imposed from above. As **Usman Haque** observes, this leaves us feeling disenfranchised. Umbrellium, the team he cofounded to design and deploy participatory platforms, is working to re-establish community engagement. Its ongoing VoiceOver project in the village of Horden, County Durham, shows how people can be encouraged to connect beyond their usual sphere and to make collective decisions, enhancing their sense of ownership of the outcomes.

Every day, almost every moment of our lives, we make decisions. We decide what to wear, where to go, what to buy (or not buy) and from where to buy it. The way we make these decisions is influenced by all manner of factors: our history, our friends and family, the advertising to which we are subjected, and even subconscious factors such as weather or mood.

As our world becomes increasingly influenced by data and networked technologies, as real-time sensor data streams from buildings, streets and mobile devices, striving to inform us about what is happening right now, and as our micro-decisions have an increasing capacity to interact with the micro-decisions of others both near and far, the complexity of making decisions, of making sense of now and the near future, and understanding the consequences of our choices becomes increasingly difficult. The volume of data, and the variety of decisions that need to be made, seem almost overwhelming. Introducing automation systems seems at first an obvious solution.

Designing Decision-Making Technologies

Automation systems such as smart thermostats help our homes decide the 'right moment' to switch on the heating, or help us manage our energy consumption. We create automation

Communication paths of the mesh-network setup were made explicit by being lit up across the neighbourhood.

systems to drive our cars, execute trades on the stock market, manage our city infrastructures, distinguish criminals within crowds or guide our economies. All of these systems deal with massive volumes of data, and the real-time complex interactions between all sorts of phenomena, much more quickly and, in a sense, more accurately than humans can. And every single one was designed. Someone somewhere, probably far away from its end users, made the most important decision of all: they decided, defined and designed the goals the system should strive for. The same individual(s), with their own perspectives and worldviews, decided on a definition for optimisation, or a definition of efficiency, safety, risk or certainty. They decided what the 'right moment', choice or consequence would be.

Decisions were also made on precisely how such parameters would be encoded into an algorithm. Essentially the set of rules used to derive a solution or make a decision, such algorithms are the primary determinants of how a system acts upon the world. The design of those rules, the selection of the inputs, the definition of the problem – collectively the goal of the system – all affect what decision is ultimately taken. Yet all too often the design of such goals and algorithms is created behind closed doors. Whether it is driverless cars, smart homes in smart cities, or curated news items in social media, other people are making countless non-consensual decisions on our behalf, in companies driven by their own commercial requirements, or organisations with their own unspoken objectives.

Who Gets to Decide What Should Be Decided Upon?

The capacity to make such crucial decisions by the people who are directly affected by them is evanescent. The idea of local decision-making, in the context of network technologies and topologies that have erased the frictions of distance, seems almost absurd.

Recently there was widespread outcry over the discovery of a faulty National Security Agency (NSA) drone-kill algorithm that may have led to thousands of people being falsely classified as dangerous, and possibly to their death. We only know this because of leaked documents. Now, not only is the decision to pull the trigger done at a distance by a faceless operator, even the decision of whom to aim at is

Conversations bounced from
home to home through the
VoiceOver network, lighting up
the 'antennae' attached outside.

We citizens need
to be involved
collectively in
helping shape the
algorithms that
govern our lives.

turned over to unaccountable technologies.

We citizens need to be involved collectively in helping shape the algorithms that govern our lives. They will affect how and where we live, and what we do from minute to minute, in the very near future. We all need to be part of the conversation, since there is no single definition of 'efficiency' or 'optimisation', or 'convenience' or 'comfort'. Or 'terrorist' for that matter.

Who is responsible for the consequences of an algorithmic decision? We hold a human responsible for how they manage a steering wheel, but if they have set their car on 'auto' and it harms someone, do we hold the engineers of the algorithm responsible? Even without automation, we still have legal arguments about chains of culpability in such situations. We are seemingly rushing into implementing opaque decision-making algorithms even though we, as humans, have yet to agree on how we should make such decisions.

As we offload more and more of our decision-making to automated processes, we begin to devalue what it is to be human, mistrusting our capacity to make important decisions.[1] We wait for 'walk' signs to tell us when to cross rather than assessing that ourselves; we ask

Google Now what the weather is rather than looking out of the window; we buy Amazon's recommendations rather than ask friends; or use sensor-filled cutlery to tell us when to stop eating. In our quest to eradicate uncertainty, we look to algorithms to tell us what to do, and then when the outcome is undesirable say 'it wasn't me, it was the data'.

Using Networked Technology to Connect and Decide Together
Beyond being control mechanisms, networked technologies are good at bridging distance: connecting people, places, things, experiences, environments and neighbourhoods to each other in real time. They help shrink the scale of the planet and make us more aware of how what we do relates to others, both human and non-human. The purpose of Umbrellium's work, therefore, is to use networked technologies not to make things more efficient or to optimise, but to see things differently so that decisions may be made together. Not to make decisions better (whatever that means), but to make them collectively; not to remove inefficiency and complexity, or iron out wrinkles and seams, but to embrace that complexity and build

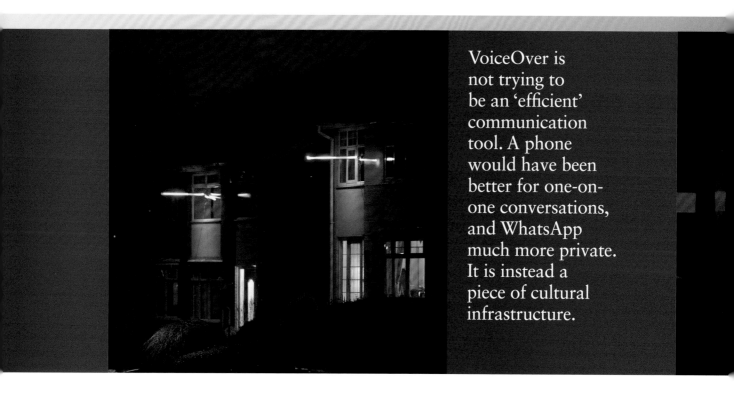

VoiceOver is
not trying to
be an 'efficient'
communication
tool. A phone
would have been
better for one-on-
one conversations,
and WhatsApp
much more private.
It is instead a
piece of cultural
infrastructure.

value from the unpredictability, serendipity and creativity that is found in messy situations. It seeks to deploy infrastructure that will be taken over and repurposed by other people so that they develop a shared sense of technological enfranchisement and ownership in civic outcomes.

An example is Umbrellium's ongoing VoiceOver project, the first phase of which was sited in the village of Horden, County Durham, in the north of England, where an interactive chain of light and sound that weaves its way around local streets was deployed in March 2016, connecting residents in ways they had never been connected before. VoiceOver is a communication network – a mesh network – that everyone can listen in on and that everyone can see. Unlike a normal telephone network, with its emphasis on privacy (an evanescent privacy according to what we know now about the NSA's deep desires), it is both hyperlocal and hyperpublic. As sound passes up and down the streets, each fragment lights up in response to the different voices and sounds passing through it, making the lines of communication explicit. Moreover, because it is designed and deployed in collaboration with local residents, its luminescent path depends on which residents have elected to host a node in the network.

VoiceOver is not trying to be an 'efficient' communication tool. A phone would have been better for one-on-one conversations, and WhatsApp much more private. It is instead a piece of cultural infrastructure – an urban systems intervention that generates new connections and creativity between different people and places. Its aim is to gather together as many people as possible at the same time, communicating with others they might not even know. In Horden, people used it to talk with each other, sing duets, recite poetry and even tell bedtime stories to the neighbourhood. Children used it to tell jokes and also to tell tales on their elder siblings.

The point was to enable local residents to become meaningfully involved in creating, installing, supporting and bringing to life a cultural infrastructure, one that actively encouraged performance, sharing and storytelling. The project enabled and in some senses required neighbours who had never talked before to communicate, and gave them an excuse to reach out. It even uncovered the fact that three cousins, who had never before all met together, had been living near to each other all along without realising it.

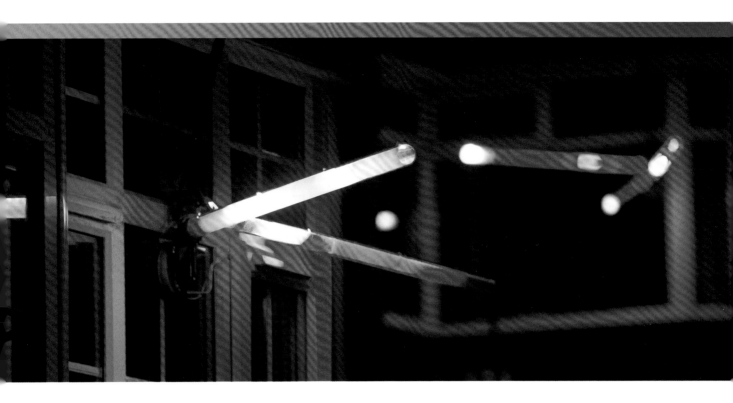

Consequences of Acting Together

The point is not that 'together' is better than 'efficient' – it simply has different outcomes. When decisions are made together, people have a greater sense of agency and accomplishment, they feel more responsibility and ownership in outcomes, and are more invested in seeing to it that things succeed.

When people act together they are more effective, and we need to encode participatory, consciously interactive parameters into our algorithms, ones that also value our communality and connectivity. As we go forward in planning for technological interventions in our cities, installing networked technologies and infrastructures for managing the complexities of our ways of life, and wiring up our homes and cars with more and more sensors, we citizens need to evaluate these systems on far more than just how efficient they are. They need to be assessed on how much they engage us in meaningful decision-making, and how much they enable us to engage with each other in making those decisions – how much they connect us together, rather than giving us reasons to stay apart.

Just as we now factor in the costs of detrimental environmental impact to economic forecasts, we should also consider the cost of disengagement and disenfranchisement in any technological deployment. As Cedric Price once said: 'Technology is the answer, but what was the question?'[2] Let us make sure we put to work the creativity of the collective, and decide those questions together, as a crowd and as a community. ⌂

Notes

1. For more on this see William Langewiesche, 'The Human Factor', *Vanity Fair*, 17 September 2014: www.vanityfair.com/news/business/2014/10/air-france-flight-447-crash.
2. Lecture delivered in 1966, available as 'Technology is the Answer, But What Was the Question?', Pidgeon Audio Visual Library and World Microfilms Publications, 1979.

Katharine Willis

Digital Neighbourhoods

Hyperlocal Village Hubs in Rural Communities

What does hyperlocal mean in a non-urban context?

Katharine Willis – Associate Professor in Digital Environments at Plymouth University's School of Art, Design and Architecture – considers what happens when rural-dwellers use technology to connect in real time both within and beyond their village, by examining a Cornwall project that has involved a series of innovative socio-digital interventions.

School of Architecture, Design and Environment, Plymouth University, Digital Neighbourhoods project, 2013–

Patterns of online and offline networks in a rural village. Central people provide dense patterns of connection, linking up the community into a dense network.

City. Technology. The two are seen as analogous. If we imagine a busy city, we see citizens plugged into smartphones and tablets connected through social media, and in offices hyperconnected through networks of work that stretch out globally. This vision of the city prioritises a globalised world, with mega urban centres. Yet much of the world's surface is predominantly rural; and even in the developed world, the rural still plays a crucial role in everyday life for many people – even if they do not actually live in rural towns or villages.

Those who live rurally have the potential to benefit most from the connectivity that the digital world brings. The vision of the rural idyll of a 'telecottage' may now be outdated, but the benefits of having a high quality of life locally whilst still being 'connected' globally still has appeal. Countering this vision is the argument that digital connectivity and online networks destroy all that is valuable about local communities, by overriding face-to-face interaction and neighbourliness. However, studies have shown that being connected online actually contributes to neighbourliness and a sense of local community. Sociologists Keith Hampton and Barry Wellman's 1999 study of 'Netville' (a pseudonym), a Toronto suburb, combined survey research with participant observation in this new 'wired-up' locality to study the impact of the Internet on local community. They found that wired residents were two to three times more likely than non-wired residents to recognise and talk with their neighbours, and that they also had more contact with friends and relatives outside the neighbourhood.[1]

Villagers' responses to the question
'What does the Internet mean to you?',
summarised on a 'post-it' board.

The aim of the Digital Neighbourhoods project was to test and understand what happens when online social networks are integrated with place-based networks.

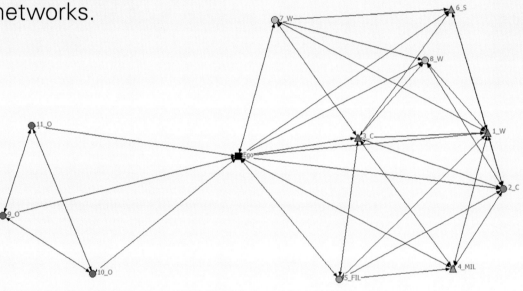

A digital village hall in the centre of the village of Pendeen, close to Land's End in Cornwall, UK, with around 900 residents. The Centre of Pendeen is a former snooker club that was refurbished and turned into a community centre which operates as a digital hub offering computer access, WiFi and digital skills training.

This contributes to what is termed 'social capital' or what the political scientist Robert Putnam has described as the 'trust, norms and networks that can improve the efficiency of society by facilitating coordinated actions'.[2] In so doing, it creates a new model of community that is not just about the geographical place. Rather, it moves towards an approach that defines community, as Barry Wellman has written, 'not in terms of locality, but as social networks of interpersonal ties that provide sociability, support, information, a sense of belonging, and social identity'.[3] So, if we return to the rural context, we have the potential for villages and towns beyond the city to become enriched by online connections that overcome some of the geographical isolation that is seen as one of the downsides of living rurally.

The aim of the Digital Neighbourhoods project undertaken by the School of Architecture, Design and Environment at Plymouth University was to test and understand what happens when online social networks are integrated with place-based networks. A particular focus was on the link between patterns of online connections and rural spatial infrastructure. The project approach put a particular focus on the spatial infrastructure that might provide a 'place' for technology, by linking up the rather ethereal world of online connections with the physical social meeting places of local communities.

Over the last three years, since the project started in 2013, the team has worked on a series of small villages in rural Cornwall, in the South West of England, as part of Superfast Cornwall Labs: a programme delivering high-speed broadband to rural communities.[4] The outcomes of a series of in-depth interviews and surveys with local people showed a pattern of connections that moved well beyond the perceived split between online connectivity and a sense of 'belonging' within a geographical place. In fact, people in rural villages primarily used their online connections to reinforce a whole range of social connections – within their neighbourhoods as well as nationally and even globally – to keep in touch with a community that extended both locally and also around the world.

The study found that connecting online was primarily a way to support village community lifestyle and to enable and extend existing connections to the village. Its methodology revealed a pattern of dense online, face-to-face and local connections through phone calls and texts that created a multilayered pattern. But it also found that some people – notably gamers – added in new connections online that were as meaningful to them as their friends and family and extended their sense of community well beyond the place where they lived.

The key 'place' for technology in a rural community is the village hall. This is the venue that, when digitally connected, can create a hyperlocal hub. Village halls are the lifeblood of rural communities: they are where people meet; they host village fairs, yoga classes, parish councils, art groups and children's parties; they build and maintain social capital. The project developed a series of digital interventions in the village halls of three rural villages in Cornwall – St Breward, Pendeen and St Dennis – to explore what happens when local people connect both within and beyond their village.

Diagram of a social network of a village inhabitant who is an active online gamer (shown at the centre as a dot). The patterns of connection reveal local connections (to the right) of family and close friends, and global connections (to the left) to online gamer friends that create another scale and locality of community.

A digital village hall link-up event. The 'hyperlocal' event created a four-way video link across Cornwall with the villages of St Breward, Pendeen and St Dennis as well as Plymouth University.

The unassuming village hall can be the 'place' where the digital, social and spatial bind together a sense of locality with the additional benefits of an online connectivity.

Facebook post about a link-up event from the Pendeen Patchwork Group.

In November 2015, an event was organised that created a digital connection simultaneously across the three Cornwall villages as well as with Plymouth, with a live video link streamed through the network. Via a four-way video conference setup, villagers in each of the village halls were able to see and talk to each other in real time. The event was deliberately embedded within the local context of the community, with a focus on the participants connecting through shared interests and thus constructing a shared space of mutual interest across the digital platform. In one village, the Pendeen Patchwork Group showcased their craft, whilst in another village the local history group explained how they had sourced and developed a book of local stories both online and offline. The potential of online live streaming is to create a sense of togetherness and reinforce locality through defining what people have in common and sharing experiences and local knowledge.

In the media's focus on what digital connectivity can bring to communities, the rural is often overlooked. This is unfortunate given that – although people never did and never will need technology to create, experience and sustain community – technology can play a valuable role in facilitating it. The unassuming village hall can be the 'place' where the digital, social and spatial bind together a sense of locality with the additional benefits of an online connectivity. This can do the vital job of enabling a sense of community that moves beyond 'community as a place' to 'community as a network' of hyperlocal connections. In our narrow focus on the digital world of hyperconnected global cities, we might potentially learn much from what it means to be locally connected in a rural village. ⌂

Notes

1. Keith Hampton and Barry Wellman, 'Neighboring in Netville: How the Internet Supports Community and Social Capital in a Wired Suburb', *City and Community*, no 2, 2003, pp 277–311.
2. Robert Putnam, 'The Prosperous Community: Social Capital and Public Life', *American Prospect*, 13, 1993, p 167.
3. Barry Wellman, 'Physical Place and Cyberplace: The Rise of Networked Individualism', in Leigh Keeble and Brian D Loader (eds), *Community Informatics: Shaping Computer-Mediated Social Relations*, Routledge (London), 2001, p 18.
4. See http://www.superfastcornwall.org/programme/research-innovation.

Moritz Behrens

Sentiment Architectures

Moritz Behrens and Konstantinos Mavromichalis,
Sentiment Cocoon,
Vivid Sydney festival of light,
Australia,
2016

A simple touch interface allowed participants to express how
they felt by how they touched. These interactions were then
transformed into pulses of light that travelled throughout the
cocoon.

as Vehicles for Participation

What if the large programmable surfaces of media architecture were used to empower citizens, instead of for commercial purposes? Designer, maker and researcher **Moritz Behrens** and his collaborators have created Sentiment Architectures with this aim in mind. Here he describes how two of their projects – the Smart Citizen Sentiment Dashboard and the Sentiment Cocoon – encourage interaction in public spaces, allowing individuals to express their feelings and enabling a better understanding of communities' needs.

Moritz Behrens
and Konstantinos
Mavromichalis,
Sentiment Cocoon,
Arup offices,
London,
2015

Sentiment Architectures are structures that unfold some form of spatial and thus temporal dimension while absorbing, reflecting or evoking human or nonhuman behaviour. 'Sentiment' is here read as both emotion and cognition.

With recent advancements in technological developments, and the declining cost of materials and infrastructure, media architecture has become an unstoppable phenomenon. Entire building facades have consequently transformed into digital walls displaying continuously dynamic content. However, large programmable surfaces need to go beyond commercial purposes, and a growing number of initiatives are now exploring how urban screens and media facades can be used for engaging with the actual needs of communities and neighbourhoods in dense cities. The EU-funded Connecting Cities Network, for example, aims to establish a global network of media facades, urban screens and projection sites to spread artistic and social content for the good of liveable future cities.[1]

Sentiment Architectures are vehicles that spark participation by designing for playful interactions mediated through interactive systems in public spaces. The approach combines ethnography-inspired workshops, iterative prototyping with digital technologies, and the deployment of architectural installations. These interactive architectural systems and tools enable citizens and inhabitants to express their feelings about local concerns, immediately and without a filter, in the public domain, the aim of which is to evoke a discourse that eventually creates a flourishing cohesive community while simultaneously informing stakeholders and policymakers. This is made possible with the growing global popularity of electronic surfaces as an architectural material.

Sentiment Architectures is not, then, a typology; it is a function that derived from a technology, sentiment analysis – a tool to identify people's emotions in language that has the potential for an expanded architectural theory and practice. As such:

Sentiment Architectures are not either positive or negative. They are part of our world. They are part of us. And that is why we have to attain a conscious understanding and handling of them.[2]

Two exemplary Sentiment Architectures have been hosted in different hyperlocal settings. The first, the Smart Citizen Sentiment Dashboard, empowered urban citizen participation by utilising landmark media facades, while the Sentiment Cocoon put the wellbeing of employees at the centre of a workplace in London, in the form of a large interactive installation. In both projects, so-called media architecture interfaces offered playful interaction modalities delivered through digital technology. Existing radio frequency identification (RFID) and its widespread use in the form of ID tags for payless travel or building access enabled participants to engage with Sentiment Dashboards and connected surfaces such as urban screens or media facades.

Smart Citizen Sentiment Dashboard
The Smart Citizen Sentiment Dashboard project was commissioned in 2013 by Galeria de Arte Digital do Sesi-SP and Verve Cultural, a partner of the Connecting Cities Network, and shown as part of the Viva Cidade Festival in São Paulo. The interactive installation allowed citizens to engage with, and comment on, the urban challenges facing their city via the media facade of the iconic Federation of Industries of the State of São Paulo (FIESP) building in the centre. During the three weeks of the festival, participants could submit their sentiments through the Sentiment Dashboard tangible interface using their RFID-enabled public transport cards and simultaneously see the effect of their actions projected onto the building's honeycomb exterior. They discussed their concerns with others next to the installation, or simply enjoyed the colourful and dynamic facade visualisation while taking pictures with their mobile phones.

Moritz Behrens
and Nina Valkanova,
Smart Citizen
Sentiment Dashboard,
São Paulo,
Brazil,
2013

above: The Sentiment Dashboard was here connected to the existing large media facade built into the honeycomb exterior of the Federation of Industries of the State of São Paulo (FIESP) building on Avenida Paulista.

below: Members of the public were invited to respond to an urban theme, such as mobility, environment, security, public space and housing, by swiping their transport cards on a custom-made device – the Sentiment Dashboard. Their unique responses were then translated into a shared visualisation and displayed instantly on the media facade connected to the dashboard.

Moritz Behrens and Nina
Valkanova, Smart Citizen
Sentiment Dashboard,
Ars Electronica
festival,
Linz, Austria,
2014

During the festival, citizens of Linz
were invited to join a workshop
to discuss the urban challenges
facing their city.

Following the success of the São Paulo installation, the Sentiment Dashboard was also shown during the Ars Electronica festival in Linz and at the Staro Riga light festival in 2014 using improved dashboards and connected to different media facades. Prior to these events, citizens of the respective neighbourhoods and cities were invited to ethnography-inspired design workshops. Participants were chosen on a first come, first served basis. The objective was to reveal socially and locally relevant topics and challenges and to gain a general understanding of the social fabric of the local communities within the cities. Attendees identified challenges such as pollution, housing, public transport or security. These topics were then translated into a culturally understandable visual language in the form of icons that was later printed onto the tangible electronic devices and programmed into the media facade visualisations.

Sentiment Cocoon

The Sentiment Cocoon proposal, initially realised in 2015, was an interactive cocoon woven out of a translucent fabric, turning the 20-metre (65-foot) high atrium at Arup's offices in Central London into a stage for social encounter. Here, employees' sentiments were collected and materialised as light and fibre, provoking mediated social interactions through an exploration of architectural form, translucent materials and responsive lighting. Via simple 'sentiment interfaces' in the form of dashboards attached to the atrium's balustrade, participants were invited to meditate on and express their mood. An algorithm fed their feelings into the system before projecting them digitally into the light field that formed the spine of the cocoon. The Sentiment Cocoon thus represented the feelings of everyone in the office building on any given day. The design intention, above all, revitalised the notion of the atrium as the social centre of a building where occupants watch, wait, rest, meet or chat.

> Employees' sentiments were collected and materialised as light and fibre, provoking mediated social interactions.

Moritz Behrens and Nina
Valkanova, Smart Citizen
Sentiment Dashboard,
Staro Riga light
festival,
Riga, Latvia,
2014

In Riga, the installation was set
up on a busy pedestrian crossing
at the intersection of Marijas
Iela and Satekles Iela, close to
the city's main train station. The
visualisation was displayed on
a large mobile screen facing
Satekles Iela, with the Sentiment
dashboard in front.

The lighting within the cocoon visually indicated the representation and physical location of the recorded sentiments and therefore the atrium space. The translucency of the material created an effect whereby the suspended Sentiment Cocoon generated a striking visual display of light informed by feelings. The objective was to design a continuous and organic cocoon-like lightweight structure that would wind up through the atrium to connect all seven floors. An adapted version was on display during the Vivid Sydney festival of light in 2016.

Empowering Citizens Through Media Architecture

The Sentiment Architectures design explorations represent an applied research into the behavioural qualities and cognitive potentials of the ever more technologically mediated urban mediascape. Media architecture installations such as the Smart Citizen Sentiment Dashboard and the Sentiment Cocoon empower citizens by allowing them to express their feelings and opinions in public – as vehicles for participation. They are attracted by the visual presence of the architectural installations, and encouraged to engage with the playful modes of interaction they offer, turning the surrounding spaces into stages for social encounter where sentiments can be discussed. ᗡ

Moritz Behrens and
Konstantinos Mavromichalis,
Sentiment Cocoon,
Arup offices,
London,
2015

The lighting design of the cocoon created an enigmatic display. Natural daylight, flowing into the atrium from the skylights above, blended with light emitted by the cocoon's spine to create rich interactions of varying forms diffused through the installation skin.

Each participant's sentiment appeared as a glowing pulse of light within the cocoon, rising to a height relating to the position of the input – the more positive the sentiment, the higher the position of the light pulse. As more people engaged with the cocoon, the combined effects of their sentiments, as a collective, became visible.

Notes
1. Susa Pop, Tanya Toft, Nerea Calvillo and Mark Wright (eds), *What Urban Media Art Can Do: Why, When, Where, and How?*, avedition (Stuttgart), 2016.
2. Moritz Behrens, Christian Berkes and Sophie Wohlgemuth (eds), *Sentiment Architectures: A Field Trip to Behaviour and Cognition in Time and Space*, botopress (Berlin), 2016.

**Will Gowland and
Samantha Lee**

UniversalAssemblyUnit,
Datum Explorer,
Sussex,
UK,
2015

A 3D point cloud captured by
a LiDAR scanner is projection-
mapped back onto itself.

△D 4D Hyperlocal Would Like to Use Your Current Location

The physical nature of current location-tracked mobile culture can open up new sites to explore our relationship to place and question our cultural reliance upon it. Recent projects by London-based multidisciplinary design studio UniversalAssemblyUnit playfully offer a shared-ownership alternative to commercially driven centralised networks. The studio's cofounders **Will Gowland and Samantha Lee** here outline three such projects, involving a weather visualiser for Alaska, a laser communication network for Mexico City and a virtual replica of woodland for East Sussex.

'Calculating Route': GMT-09:05. You are stuck in traffic on Old Street roundabout in Shoreditch, East London, surrounded by a flurry of Ubers. Outdoor advertising company JCDecaux's massive LED screens suggest a cafe nearby, four-star rated and five minutes' walk away. Trending on Google search is Arsenal versus Barcelona; the weather is 6°C (42.8°F), mostly sunny.

Google's digital campaign occupying Old Street roundabout is a monument to the hyperlocal, one where place and time have come to define the content of our movements and physical interactions with the city. Described as 'iconic advertising architecture', it has become synonymous with the 'Silicon Roundabout' technology hub of Shoreditch.

Thanks to an array of mobile apps that rely on location data, placing ourselves in the world is more egocentric than ever before. The hyperlocal is less of a postcode, but stems from a device we carry around in our pockets. It is a context governed by the smallprint of our carrier's Privacy and Location Services, where our movements become a valuable commodity for big-data companies. This personalised mobile experience is a source of familiarity to navigate the world. Uber's logo redesign, for example, attempts to reflect the individuality of local markets by using 65 country-specific colour and pattern palettes and five global ones.[1] These mood boards appear to be pieced together from page one of a Google image search, regurgitating a superficial representation of place.

If the emerging hyperlocal is to foster any meaningful sense of a past local culture, one that emerges organically through physical proximity and everyday social interactions, it needs to develop via a bottom-up approach, whereby our mobile experiences are not purely directed by global companies like Google, Facebook and Uber. The controversy surrounding such companies is often that their ability to operate outside the rules and regulations of local government means they do not take responsibility for nurturing local culture. A viable alternative to such commercially driven centralised networks is the emergence of mesh networks, creating off-grid communication infrastructures that foster a greater sense of community through their shared ownership and operation. Significant for their use of wireless technology in a decentralised mode of governance, they negate the need for a single body or company to manage and control the system.

Underpinning the cultural reliance on top-down global firms is an ageing Global Positioning System (GPS) infrastructure, a constellation of satellites orbiting earth approximately 20,200 kilometres (12,550 miles) away. GPS was the first Global Navigation Satellite System (GNSS), launched in 1978 by the US government. The carefully synchronised motion of the satellites with the earth's rotation provides us with varying levels of resolution, accuracy and accessibility. Tracking our every movement, a personalised dataset of our virtual footprint is evolving, sending us ever more bespoke push notifications. The world is now concealed and manipulated in ways that make answering the question of 'where am I?' an impossibility. Glitches in the big and fragile infrastructures of GPS mean we are sometimes both here and there, as a pulsing blue dot locates us to within 50 metres (164 feet).

The three projects illustrated here, by London-based cross-disciplinary think-and-do tank UniversalAssemblyUnit, explore the physical nature of GPS and real-time locating systems as new sites to provoke our relationship to place, communication and social interaction.

UniversalAssemblyUnit.
Silicon Roundabout Instagram post,
London,
2016

Google's digital advertising sits as a monument
to the hyperlocal on Old Street roundabout.

Here Be Dragons
[71.2906° N, 156.7886° W: Barrow, Alaska]

Our first scenario begins in the far North, a vast and featureless territory where shipping companies, climate scientists and inuit alike rely heavily on GPS for navigation. In this context, Here Be Dragons (2012) takes the form of a live GPS visualisation app, a working prototype that aims to highlight how this invisible layer of data can have physical consequences in the real world. By spoofing and jamming the GPS network, real-time data is used to generate a local virtual topography that reflects the stability and reliability of the data it receives. Journeying through this landscape with your trusted GNSS receiver, you get lost in a wilderness of illegal signal-jamming formations. Virtual protest icebergs drift through the autonomously navigated oil-shipping lanes, launched by Greenpeace in an attempt to disrupt operations.

In the perpetual darkness you encounter this alternative virtual topography, a territorial architecture of spoofed cartography that operates in both the physical and virtual domains. Some are landscapes of misdirection, others navigational markers guiding you safely through this unstable terrain. It is in these contested waters that the consequences of relying on such systems is laid bare. Through the peaks and troughs of the visualisation app, providing a GPS weather forecast of sorts, you begin to relate to this data as intuitively as you do the weather.

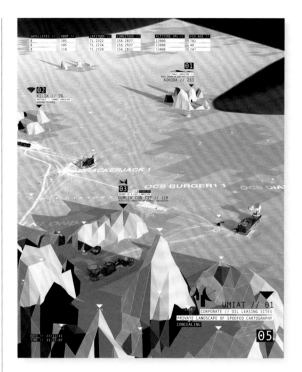

UniversalAssemblyUnit,
Here Be Dragons,
Barrow, Alaska, 2012

above:
In-app GPS weather visualiser. Custom-built software
visualises the invisible landscape of GPS.

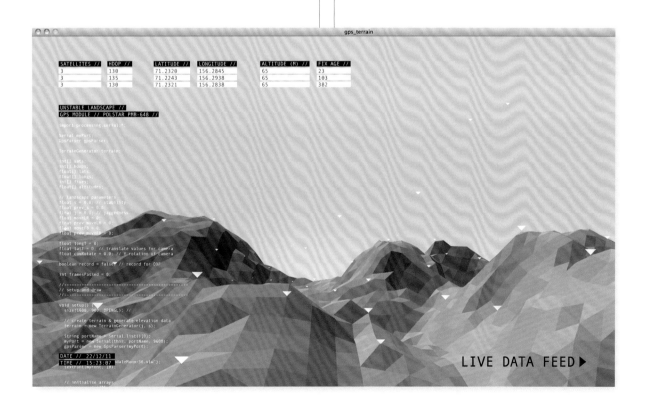

Film still.
Spoofed GPS cartographies conceal
illegal oil-drilling activities.

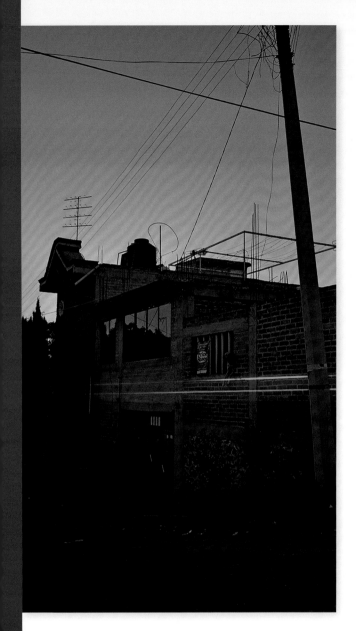

UniversalAssemblyUnit,
Off Grid,
Mexico City,
2013

Film still. An off-grid laser communication
network active in the favelas of Mexico City.

Off Grid
[23.6345° N, 102.4428° W: Mexico City]

As you step off the plane, your phone automatically switches time zone courtesy of the GPS network's synchronised atomic clock. Wandering the side streets of Mexico City, among the web of power lines and redundant telephone cables, you catch fleeting glimpses of faint laser lines. These are part of the speculative Off Grid (2013) local telecommunications project developed to circumnavigate the monopoly of centralised communication and navigation systems such as GPS. Using lasers to transmit audio and data without the need for hard infrastructures, this resilient and ad-hoc network consists of a series of transceivers and mirror relays along which travel off-grid conversations, weaving through streets and around corners as they automatically re-route to maintain uninterrupted dialogue.

Creating its own circadian rhythms, the night's sky is illuminated by the pulsing laser lights of a city in visible conversation. It is in this era of open source that the sharing economy has created the platform from which to produce and create the toolkits to build and self-govern from the ground up, through off-grid networks, experiments and phenomena.

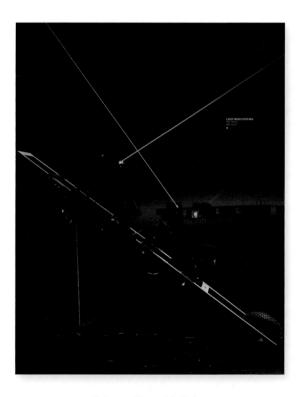

UniversalAssemblyUnit,
Off Grid installation,
London,
2013

Prototype for an off-grid communication
system using point-to-point laser transceivers
and mirror relays.

As you
step off the plane,
your phone automatically
switches time zone
courtesy of the GPS
network's synchronised
atomic clock.

Datum Explorer
[50.9174° N, 0.4837° E: Sussex, UK]

You are driving to your Airbnb, booked for the weekend in the English countryside, navigating via the 'quietest route'. On the way, a notification on your phone tells you there is an interesting detour to be made, highly rated on TripAdvisor and personally selected based on your location and search activity: 'Welcome to Sussex! You are 1 mile away from a destination recommended for you. Please take the next left to enter Great Park Farm. Swipe for details.' You have reached the site of Datum Explorer (2014), a multiplatform art project and installation that allows you to explore a virtual replica of the local woodland on your mobile device.

Using a light detection and ranging (LiDAR) scanner and binaural recording device, a 3D dataset has been captured to millimetre accuracy and positioned in geographical space using longitude and latitude. Sensing your proximity, the forest explodes into a colourful bloom as you trigger a geofence, a virtual perimeter for this real-world geographical location. Upon launching the Datum Explorer app, you encounter a landscape strangely familiar to the one you are standing in, but occupied by digital flora and fauna. The project is conditioned by the new hyperlocal, one enmeshed in geographically relevant data from the specificity of the point cloud to your GPS location. As your digital footprint evolves, it fuses with the natural world.

Detours Through the Hyperlocal

In a city such as London, we find ourselves immersed in a commercially driven culture of the hyperlocal. By understanding the technologies and infrastructures that facilitate this emerging urban condition, they can be reappropriated to better suit user needs. Emerging toolsets such as Here Be Dragons, Off Grid and Datum Explorer are opening up parallel sites for interventions that can be playful, fantastical and alternative, evolving the narrative of the hyperlocal by creating local microclimates of cultural phenomena akin to meteorological events. ⌂

Note
1. Jessi Hempel, 'The Inside Story of Uber's Radical Rebranding', *Wired*, 2 February 2016: www.wired.com/2016/02/the-inside-story-behind-ubers-colorful-redesign.

above:
In-app visualisation.
A virtual replica of the forest bursts into bloom.

UniversalAssemblyUnit, Datum Explorer,
Sussex, UK, 2015

A multiplatform art installation that allows users to access a
virtual replica of local woodland on their mobile device.

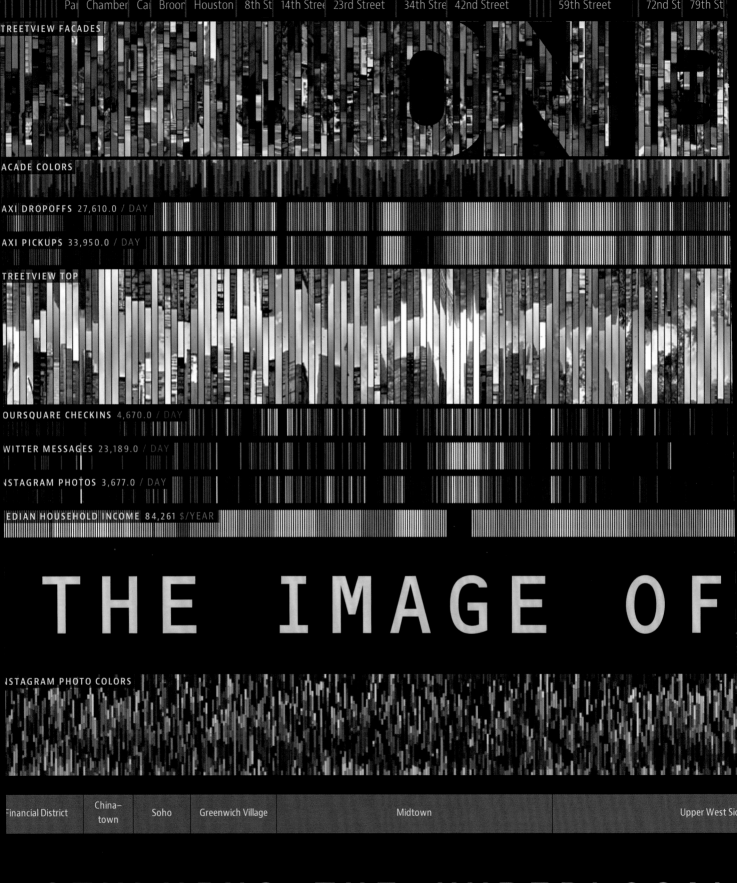

TREETVIEW FACADES

ACADE COLORS

AXI DROPOFFS 27,610.0 / DAY

AXI PICKUPS 33,950.0 / DAY

TREETVIEW TOP

OURSQUARE CHECKINS 4,670.0 / DAY

WITTER MESSAGES 23,189.0 / DAY

NSTAGRAM PHOTOS 3,677.0 / DAY

EDIAN HOUSEHOLD INCOME 84,261 $/YEAR

THE IMAGE OF

NSTAGRAM PHOTO COLORS

Financial District | China–town | Soho | Greenwich Village | Midtown | Upper West Sid

STUDYING THE HYPERLOCAL

Lev Manovich and Agustin Indaco

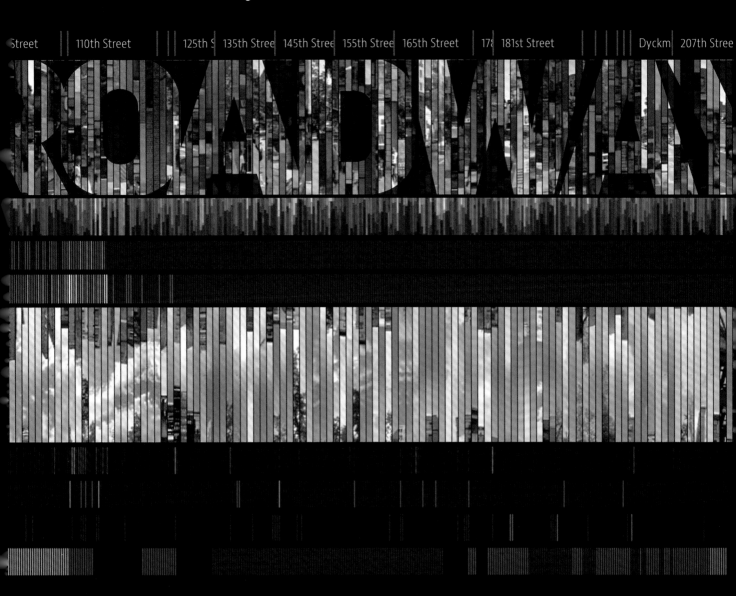

ROADWAY

A DATA CITY

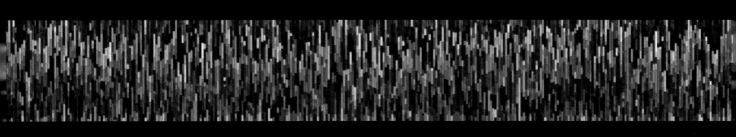

| Morningside Heights | Harlem | Hamilton Heights | Washington Heights | Fort George | Inwood |

WITH SOCIAL MEDIA

Sharing photos, videos and comments on social media may seem an idle pastime, but it is not without its uses where urban design is concerned. Analysing such posts can yield helpful indicators as to how people experience the built environment. **Lev Manovich and Agustin Indaco**, of the Software Studies Lab at the University of California, San Diego and the Graduate Center, City University of New York, here outline two of the Lab's recent research projects, which have involved examining extensive Instagram data from various cities around the globe.

Social media content, such as Instagram images, their tags and descriptions, is now a key form of contemporary city life. It tells people where the activities and locations that interest them are, and allows them to share their urban experiences and self-representations. It creates an 'image of a city' for its residents and for the outside world. The identity of any city today is as much composed of the media content shared in that city via social networks as of its infrastructure and economic activities, and must therefore be considered in any urban analysis.

Computational analysis of large numbers of user-generated photos and videos shared in particular areas can also help us to understand how people experience architecture and urban structures and what they do there. This can be carried out at any scale, from the city to the hyperlocal level of streets, buildings or parts of interiors. The proportion of all shared Instagram photos that show the built environment can be compared for different cities, alongside an analysis of which observation points for landmarks are the most popular, and what emotions they evoke depending on the time of the day. These patterns can then be compared for residents and for tourists, for different genders, age and so on. In short being able to analyse digital traces of what large numbers of people do in our built environments and how they see and use them can be very useful for urban design.

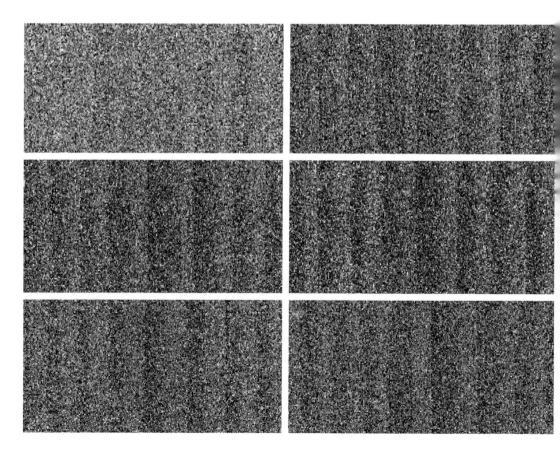

Software Studies Lab
(Lev Manovich
and Jay Chow),
Selfiecity,
University of
California,
San Diego and
Graduate Center,
City University
of New York,
2013–16

Comparison of Instagram activity in different cities (left to right, from top left): Bangkok, Berlin, Moscow, New York, São Paolo and Tokyo. Each visualisation shows 20,000 images shared consequently over one week in the given city.

In 2012, research teams at the Software Studies Lab at the University of California, San Diego and the Graduate Center, City University of New York began analysing over 16 million Instagram photos shared in 17 global cities. The teams included data scientists, software developers, data visualisation designers, media theorists, art historians, economists and urban designers. Starting with a general comparison of 2.3 million images shared in 13 global cities, the research consequently focused on more specific types of images filtered by content, such as self-portraits (Selfiecity, 2014), a particular street (On Broadway, 2014), or a combination of city area and time period (for example, the centre of Kiev during the Maidan revolution of 2014 in the Exceptional and the Everyday project).[1]

While the work of the Software Studies Lab shows how social media content can be useful for understanding the hyperlocal, it also reveals the limitations of this type of data. In many central urban areas, social media has very high spatial and temporal resolution. For the Inequaligram project (2016), the Lab collected all 7,442,454 geocoded Instagram photos publicly shared in Manhattan over six months from March to August 2014. In a single 3,000-square-metre (32,300-square-foot) area of Times Square, Instagram users shared 43,541 images in this period. However, in many other areas of Manhattan, only a few dozen images were shared during the same five months. Such low density in many parts of cities therefore limits the usefulness of social media. Another limitation is the demographic of social media users; for example, in many world cities only younger, well-educated people may post content. So, while in some cases social media is a great resource for studying hyperlocal locations, in other cases direct observation or surveys may be better at capturing patterns in how people use the city. Large-scale computational urban social media analysis can therefore only supplement, as opposed to replace, other research methods for urban design and architecture.

On Broadway

On Broadway focused on this single, very long street (21 kilometres/13.5 miles) that crosses all Manhattan, as well as a slightly wider area than the street itself to capture activities nearby. To define these areas, the researchers divided Broadway into 30-metre (98-foot) long segments, and selected 100-metre (328-foot) wide rectangle areas around each of these, resulting in 713 identical areas across which social media images and other characteristics could be compared.

The main goal of the project was to construct a novel mechanism for navigating a 'data city' consisting of many layers of images and information – an alternative way of visualising urban structures and activities without the use of maps, graphs and numbers. The result is a new visual metaphor for

Software Studies Lab (Daniel Goddemeyer, Moritz Stefaner, Dominikus Baur and Lev Manovich), On Broadway, University of California, San Diego and Graduate Center, City University of New York, 2014

Graph comparing the data layers used to represent Broadway, projected onto a horizontal axis (south to north becomes left to right). Graph height at each location corresponds to volume of data.

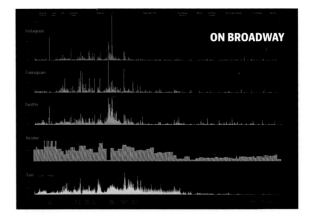

Below top: The project combines an interactive installation and a website. A screenshot from the installation, at full zoom-out, shows the entire length (21 kilometres/13 miles) of Broadway in Manhattan. The installation was exhibited at the New York Public Library, which commissioned the project, from December 2014 to January 2016.

Below middle: Neighbourhood-level view showing the Midtown area in Manhattan.

Below bottom: Block-level view of Times Square.

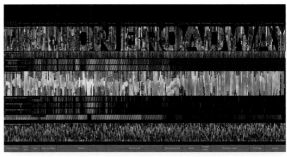

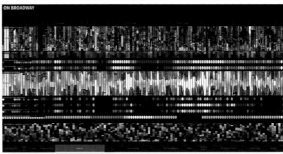

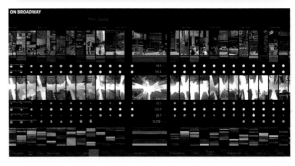

thinking about the city, a visually rich, image-centric interface, with a vertical stack of image and data layers where numbers play only a secondary role. There are 13 such layers, all aligned to locations along Broadway, including images shared on Instagram and Twitter, from Google Street View, Foursquare 'check-ins', taxi rides, and selected economic and social indicators from the US Census. Overall, over 30 million data points and images were used to represent activities along a single street.

Moving along the representation of Broadway, users see a selection of Instagram photos from each area, left, right, and top Google Street View images, as well as the average number of taxi pickups and drop-offs, Twitter posts with images, and average family income for the parts of the city crossed by Broadway. To help with navigation, additional layers were added showing the names of Manhattan neighbourhoods, cross-streets and landmarks.

This multi-layered Broadway 'corridor' can be explored at many scales. Zooming out reveals all 21 kilometres (13.5 miles) of the street, displayed as narrow vertical slices of every Google Street View photo. Zooming in, the slices become wider until the image of the selected area is shown at full size. The visuals in all layers, and numbers showing aggregated activity, are instantly updated when the user moves right or left, or changes zoom level.

The volumes of all data layers have a strong correlation, as can be seen on a graph plotting the volumes of all of the variables the Software Studies Lab examined. The variables have a strong positive correlation; their values go up and down together. In this 'correlated city', the social inequality and digital divide are now joined by a social media divide that is even more extreme. In affluent areas, people make more money, take taxis, and post more images on Instagram and Twitter. In poorer areas, they make less money, rarely use taxis, and post many fewer images on social networks.

Inequaligram

The Lab's next project, Inequaligram, resulted from further exploration of the connections revealed by On Broadway by looking at the characteristics of Instagram posts and US Census socioeconomic indicators for Manhattan.

The US Census reports aggregate socioeconomic characteristics of populations using a type of division called 'tracts'. There are 287 census tracts in Manhattan, the average population of each is between 3,000 and 4,000, and average size is 0.36 square kilometers (0.14 square miles). The Inequaligram project used these tract areas to compare patterns in Instagram sharing and indicators such as income, rent, education level and unemployment rate.

The Software Studies Lab project team selected Instagram for this analysis because it has the strongest geographic and spatial identity of all social

Software Studies Lab (Agustin Indaco and Lev Manovich), Inequaligram, University of California, San Diego and Graduate Center, City University of New York, 2016

Locations of Instagram images shared by New York City visitors (left) and locals (right). Each map uses a 100,000 random image sample drawn from the larger set of 7,442,454 geotagged images publicly shared in Manhattan from March to August 2014.

media services. While tweets and Facebook posts do also have geo-coordinates and discuss local events at the moment of the user's posting, Instagram images often directly capture these events and show users in particular places. The images, videos, date and time metadata, descriptions and hashtags allow collective representations of city life along these separate dimensions to be studied. For example, the number of images shared between areas, the different subjects represented, the most popular and most unique hashtags, how people are dressed and so on can all be compared, and extracted automatically using data-science techniques available in open-source software.

In contrast to other social media services, the image- and location-driven format of Instagram creates an image of a city for both locals and visitors. It is therefore useful for architects, urban designers and planners to understand what such collective

representations contain, and how their characteristics are related to both a city's architectural structures (for example, presence of tourist landmarks) and socioeconomic social structures (for example, the locations of rich/poor areas).

Urban planners and architects know how to map the physical structures of cities, but what are the most informative ways for them to map and analyse social media? In a city such as New York, people share a very large number of Instagram images in some areas and very few in others, and some may include more hashtags and descriptions of local architecture than are posted elsewhere. Plotting such characteristics of users' posts using their geolocations reveals that their spatial distributions are very uneven.

To be able to quantify exactly how uneven these distributions are, the Inequaligram team developed a new concept of 'social media inequality' that allows quantitative comparison of spatial patterns in relevant social media activity between parts of a city, a number of cities, or any other spatial areas. The concept was defined using an analogy with that of economic inequality, which indicates how economic characteristics or material resources such as income, wealth or consumption are distributed within a city, country or between countries. Accordingly, social media inequality indicates how various characteristics of shared social media content are distributed between geographic areas: for example, number of photos shared by all users of a social network in a given city area, numbers of hashtags, and numbers of unique hashtags.

The Instagram data was normalised to compensate for differences in the geographic size of tracts, and dates of shared images were used to estimate whether a particular user lives in Manhattan or is only visiting. According to these estimates, the project dataset contains 5,918,408 million images from 366,539 unique Instagram accounts of local residents, and 1,524,046 images from 505,345 accounts that belong to visitors. To compare social media inequality across Manhattan for these two groups, Inequaligram employed the Gini index, commonly used to measure economic inequality. In the case of Instagram, if people were to share exactly the same number of images each, in each city tract, this represents complete equality, and Gini index = 0. If, on the other hand, all images are shared in only one tract, and nothing in all other tracts, this constitutes complete inequality, and Gini index = 1.

Inequaligram found that the Gini index for numbers of images shared in Manhattan between all tracts is 0.494 for locals, and 0.669 for visitors. For the total numbers of tags, the index is even higher: 0.514 for locals, and 0.678 for visitors. To put this into context, Instagram inequality for numbers of visitors' images in Manhattan (Gini = 0.669) is larger than income inequality in the most unequal country in the world (Seychelles, where Gini = 0.658). Social media shared by locals has a Gini coefficient similar to countries that rank between 25 and 30 in the list of countries by income inequality, such as Costa Rica (0.486), Mexico (0.481) and Ecuador (0.466).

But what factors drive high inequality of Instagram sharing between parts of Manhattan? In the case of visitors, they share most images in Midtown Manhattan (with its large retail zones and many hotels), around famous landmarks such as Times Square and the Flatiron Building, and in the evening areas like East Village and the Lower East Side with their many restaurants and bars. In the case of locals, analysis suggests that differences in their social media activity are to a large extent driven by commuting patterns. During working hours on weekdays, the residents of less affluent areas such as parts of Manhattan north of 100th Street work in more prosperous areas of the city – those below

Proportion of images shared by locals in selected Manhattan neighbourhoods south of 59th Street for every hour in a 24-hour cycle. The graph uses time stamps of 5,918,408 million images shared by 366,539 local residents.

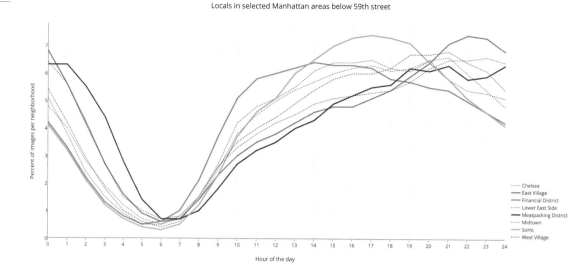

Proportion of images shared by visitors in selected Manhattan neighbourhoods south of 59th Street for every hour in a 24-hour cycle. The graph uses time stamps of 1,524,046 images shared by 505,345 visitors.

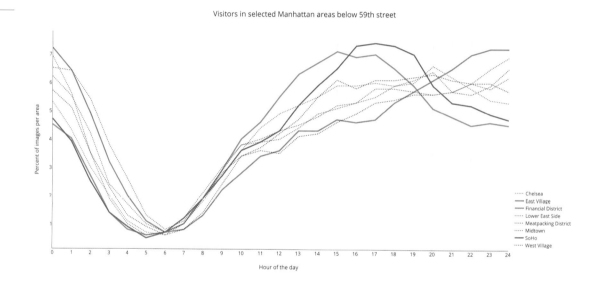

Proportion of images shared by locals in selected Manhattan neighbourhoods above 59th Street for every hour in a 24-hour cycle. The graph uses time stamps of 5,918,408 million images shared by 366,539 local residents.

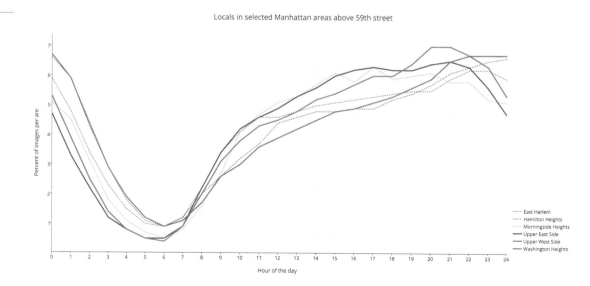

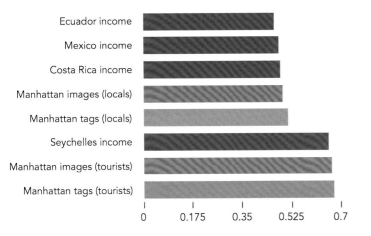

Gini inequality measure for numbers of Instagram images and tags shared in Manhattan compared to income inequality measures in selected countries.

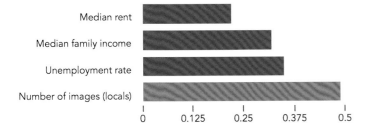

Gini inequality measures for Instagram images shared by locals in 287 Manhattan tracts of land, and selected Census economic indicators (rent, income, unemployment) for the same tracts. 'Tracts' are spatial divisions used by US Census. Gini measures for economic indicators are calculated using 2014 Census data.

The social media layer plays a very important role by filtering the city in particular ways, highlighting some locations and making others invisible.

100th Street, and particularly in Midtown. This is where they share images on Instagram during the day, so their posts are added to these areas.

Looking at inequality patterns of Instagram posts shared by locals and visitors together, it was found that the areas of Manhattan below 100th Street with most businesses are also those that are the most popular among visitors. We thus have the effect of 'double amplification' – social media contributions by affluent residents from these areas are amplified by the contributions of people who commute there for work from other parts of Manhattan, and also by out-of-city visitors. Comparing social media statistics with Census indicators for tracts in Manhattan, the inequality of number of Instagram images between tracts is bigger than inequalities in levels of income, rent and unemployment. Gini indexes are 0.32 (median income), 0.22 (median rent), 0.35 (unemployment rate), and 0.49 (number of Instagram images shared by local residents) – an unexpected and troubling finding. This means that the larger part of Manhattan has very little or no representation on Instagram. Additional data analysis quantifies this inequality in a different way: 50 per cent of all images by locals were shared in only 21 per cent of Manhattan areas. And for visitors, 50 per cent of their images were shared in only 12 per cent of Manhattan areas.

Reading the Hyperlocal

Social media's big data offers many more analytical possibilities for urban researchers, planners and architects besides those discussed here. By downloading, analysing and visualising user-shared photos, along with their tags, descriptions, time stamps and geo-coordinates, the Software Studies Lab has pieced together a collective image of a city to see how it changes over time. The concept of social media inequality has allowed measurement of how this image changes from area to area, and comparison of such images at arbitrary spatial scales.

The hyperlocal certainly contains more layers than social media alone. And yet, as suggested, the social media layer plays a very important role by filtering the city in particular ways, highlighting some locations and making others invisible. By analysing large sets of posts and images from sites such as Instagram as in the On Broadway and Inequaligram projects, the effects of this filtering can be understood and compared across a single city or many thousands. ⌂

Note
1. See Lev Manovich, Alise Tifentale, Mehrdad Yazdani and Jay Chow, 'The Exceptional and the Everyday: 144 Hours in Kyiv', *IEEE Big Data 2014 Conference Proceedings*, Washington DC, 2014, and http://www.the-everyday.net/.

Check–In

1 Foto

Foursquare and the Rich Annotated Topology of Citizen-Generated Hyperlocal Data

Over the last few years, a new resource has emerged for studying the evolution of specific cities. That resource is urban annotation: the attachment of comments to places so that they can later be accessed by others in that same location via smartphone. The city guide app Foursquare is the prime example of this. Barcelona-based curator and cultural researcher **José Luis de Vicente** examines the app from its origins to the types of data it generates, considering its implications and its surprisingly accurate predictive potentials.

Duck & Waffle
restaurant,
Heron Tower,
London

The Foursquare city guide app deepens urban knowledge by featuring recommendations from visitors to make trips to a wider range of places, some of them unexpected, such as the 24/7 restaurant on the 40th floor of the Heron Tower, the highest in London.

It is 29 February 2016, and we are having lunch on the 40th floor of the Heron Tower, in London's financial district. We were supposed to enjoy the impressive views, but, being honest, I am enjoying more my father's befuddled expression as the waiter brings him his unexpectedly peculiar order – a duck confit leg on top of a waffle. We did not end up here on the last day of this vacation trip because we bumped into the place, of course, and we were not told to come by any friend or restaurant guide. Actually, the recommendation algorithm suggested us to.

The sequence that placed us here went something like this. Determined to get my parents to try some contemporary British food during their holiday, I search for 'gastropubs' on the Foursquare city guide app, from the namesake location intelligence company with more than 50 million monthly active users across its three apps and websites. A couple of options appear, none of them fully convincing. But while contemplating one of the suggestions, I notice an additional list of places at the bottom of the screen, presented as 'similar' to the one I am currently reading. One of them shows up as having been visited by a couple of local friends whose criteria I definitely trust. A few hours later we get to the unlikely gastropub 40 floors up in the London sky.

We are here because a couple of people were here before, and because they actively and consciously expressed their presence with a 'check-in', the Foursquare term for the action of establishing your location in a particular spot of a city, on a particular day and time (now this functionality appears in the Swarm app, while Foursquare is for local discovery). Their reasons for expressing their presence here sometime in the past, creating a log into a structured dataset, are not obvious; a Foursquare check-in can be a note to yourself in case you want to remember the name of that place you went to once. It can be a real-time notification to your list of contacts, in case anyone is nearby and wants to meet; it can even be a way of producing a memento of a memory, a mechanism to trigger the remembrance of that particular meal during that holiday trip. In any case, that action was catalogued and preserved so that it has the capacity of triggering other actions by other people in the future. Urban data, and data produced by citizens, can have powerful affordances.

'Check-in' is the Foursquare term for establishing your location in a particular spot of a city, on a particular day and time, a functionality that now appears in the Swarm app, while Foursquare is for local discovery.

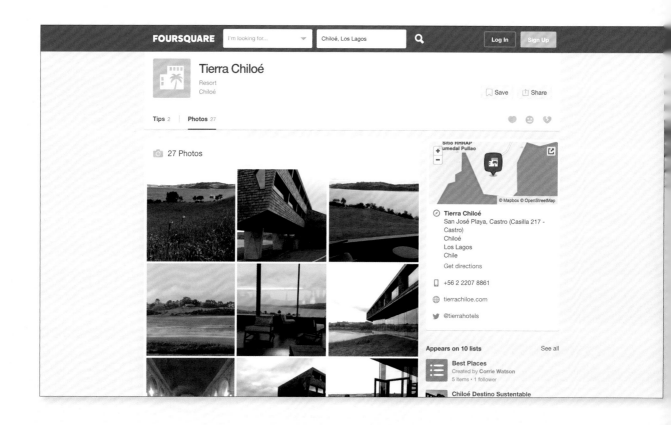

The Hyper-Surveyed City and the Fabric of Hyperlocal Data

Like all complex contemporary systems, cities are today being excruciatingly surveyed through data and reproduced in data from every angle. Up high in orbit, they are photographed to produce high-resolution satellite imagery, and scanned from planes with lasers to create colourful light detection and ranging (LiDAR) models. On the ground, they are observed by the nine eyes of Google cars, capturing not only the image of every number of every street, but also as many service set identifier (SSID) names of WiFI networks as they can find, to improve the accuracy of GPS location. Moving vehicles are tracked so that we can have accurate, up-to-the-minute information on the arrival of the next bus, or how easy it will be to find a taxi or Uber. Credit-card transactions or phone calls on the streets are scrutinised to improve the stability of those services or even to understand the ethnic diversity of a neighbourhood.

But some of the richest information being produced about cities today is the hyperlocal data that citizens are creating every time someone takes their phone and makes a mark on a data-driven service, assigning some text, image or video to geographic coordinates, with the intention of saying 'I am here' or 'this happened here'. Thanks to location technologies for mobile phones, place is a variable that is regularly included in most of the information objects that we are invited to produce in social services. Tweets and Facebook posts can be pinned to a position, as well as Instagram pictures, Periscope video streams and many other kinds of social media objects. In other cases, location is not an optional add-on to a piece of media, but the defining characteristic of the object itself. The most notable case of this are comments in travel and restaurant guides and services, from TripAdvisor to Yelp.

The irony is that once we discarded the outdated notion of cyberspace as a naive characterisation of our relationship to information – where the digital was somehow considered a parallel, alternative dimension to physical reality – we started to attach mountains of intangible information to every coordinate in space. Restaurants, bus stops, statues, fountains, airport gates – any noticeable point of reference in a city has likely been defined by a user of a hyperlocal application, given an identifiable name, and used to attach pictures, comments or videos to it. This rich fabric of hyperlocal data generated by citizens is stored in data

Christopher Allen, Brian House and Jesse Shapins, Yellow Arrow, New York City, 2004

Left: This Yellow Arrow street-art project pioneered geolocal mapping. Participants placed uniquely coded Yellow Arrow stickers and sent an SMS message that could be received and responded to by others visiting the site. This location-based exchange could be extended by participants annotating arrows with photos and maps on the Yellow Arrow website.

Proboscis, Urban Tapestries Symbian smartphone app, 2003–4

At a time when apps were just starting to emerge, Alice Angus and Giles Lane, the founders of independent artist-led creative studio Proboscis, investigated through their Urban Tapestries project how GIS and mobile technologies could help people to map and share their knowledge, experience, stories and information, and created a mobile platform for public authoring.

centres and accessed through a combination of smartphones, apps, GPS and WiFi signals. And the service that pushed forward this vision and made it common was undoubtedly Foursquare.

The Dream and the Vision of the Geospatial Web

Place-specific media objects became possible in the early 2000s, with the popularisation and miniaturisation of location technologies like GPS. The Locative Media movement – a loose conglomeration of academics, human–computer interface researchers and new media artists – explored how the vocabulary of interaction would be transformed by the simple act of including geographical position as one of the variables that the programmer or designer of an application could use.

Of all the possibilities this opportunity offered, one of the most seductive was that of urban annotation. A strategy with Situationist echoes, urban annotation involved attaching memories, stories and comments to places in space so that they could be later retrieved by any other user in those same coordinates through the use of a smartphone. Many experimental platforms and art projects in the first half of the decade played with this scenario, from Proboscis's Urban Tapestries (2004), using personal digital assistants (PDAs) and Symbian mobile phones, to the much simpler street-art project Yellow Arrow staged in 2004 on the Lower East Side of Manhattan (Christopher Allen, Brian House and Jesse Shapins, growing to include participants in 38 countries around the world), where arrow-shaped stickers with unique identifier numbers were placed in any spot on a street. SMS messages with thoughts and memories could be attached to the ID of the sticker and later retrieved by any passer-by who encountered the 'yellow arrow'. These early examples of what then was called the 'Geospatial Web' hinted at the possibilities mobile technologies could offer to create a rich information topology of the city.

Place-specific media objects became possible in the early 2000s, with the popularisation and miniaturisation of location technologies like GPS.

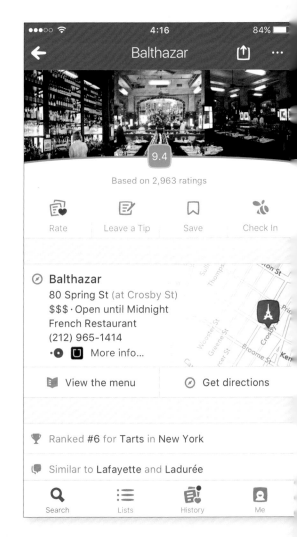

To reach critical mass, though, wide adoption by users would require new kinds of devices, with accurate location, stable broadband data and more sophisticated input mechanisms than the clunky keyboards of mobile phones. The introduction of the first-generation iPhone in 2007 convinced locative media designers and developers that the technical platform required to create a geospatial web with potentially millions of users was finally ready. The best-positioned of them all to create what would become the by-default urban annotation service turned out to be Dennis Crowley, a graduate of New York University's Interactive Telecommunications Program (ITP).

Crowley's thesis project at ITP was an SMS-based location service that would help urbanite technophiles to introduce some artificial serendipity into their social lives. Dodgeball – the name of the project – allowed users to notify their location in real time to their designated friends on the service. The expectation would be that casual encounters could actually be stimulated by letting friends be aware of each other's movements around the city. The idea was intriguing enough that Google bought Crowley's project – and his talent – in 2005. This promising start led to basically nothing for Dodgeball, and two years later Crowley would leave the search-engine giant, frustrated by their lack of interest in developing the application further. The timing was about right, since this would leave him time to launch a new location-based service in time for the age of the iPhone.

Foursquare Catalogue of Urban Data

Launched in 2009, Foursquare would keep Dodgeball's social dimension by allowing you to communicate your position in the city to your contacts on the network, in real time. The way of doing this was by 'checking in' on a spot chosen among a list of suggested locations. The locations list would be generated by the device choosing those spots closest to the current coordinates. And the list of spots would not be defined by Foursquare itself: any user could create a new location, whether it was a bar, a restaurant or cafe, a library or a film theatre. In addition to allowing you to establish your position on the spots, comments could be added to any of the places. Along with Dodgeball's location notification service, Foursquare was also now an excruciatingly detailed and annotated index of urban locations.

Foursquare's community of users, now across its three apps and websites, have been producing three kinds of hyperlocal data. The first are the check-ins, the act of placing themselves in a specific location. The check-in became a feature that would later be reproduced by most social web services, from Facebook to Instagram, which relied on Foursquare's user-generated index of locations until it was bought by Facebook in 2012.

w and opposite: The square app enables you to municate your position in y to your contacts on the ork in real time by checking n a spot chosen from a list of ested locations generated he device that selects those s closest to the current dinates.

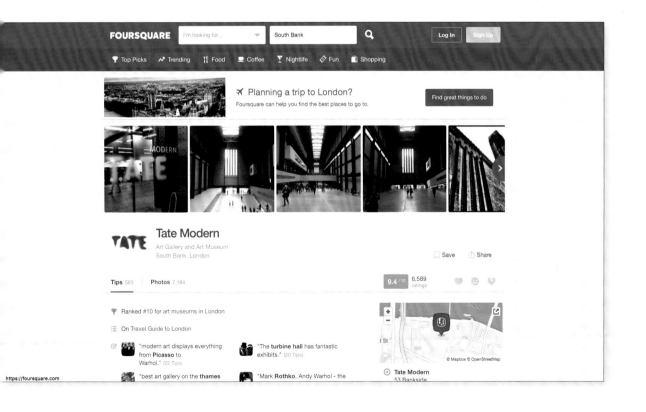

The second kind of hyperlocal data is, of course, the index of locations themselves, estimated to contain around 85 million different places. This crowdsourced data is one of the main resources the Foursquare community has produced, and one key asset for Crowley's company. Foursquare sells to third parties the right to get access to their location database, and it has been used by over 100,000 developers in their own applications, among them popular services like Pinterest, Twitter, and Microsoft's AI personal assistant, Cortana. The fact that the everyday activity of Foursquare users keeps the database relevant and up to date is one of its main attractions, and a superb example of how Silicon Valley's cognitive capitalism has turned something as mundane as updating the name of a restaurant into an exploitable form of labour.

The third type of hyperlocal data are the comments that people add to locations; tips on what to order at a restaurant, or what not to miss at a museum. These have become so valuable that they are now a core element of the Foursquare city guide app. In 2014, the company split its single app into two: now Swarm is where users check in and compete for mayorships and to win the leaderboard. Since 2009, Foursquare has gathered close to 10 billion check-ins; it now captures more than 8 million per day on Swarm. However, the future of the platform, both for Foursquare's 50 million monthly active users and for its business model, is the location intelligence that helps guide millions of people as they move through the world. Another new technology that makes this possible is Pilgrim, which has run in the background of Foursquare and Swarm since 2014.

Pilgrim tries to determine your location every time you stop moving, even if you do not actually check in at a place, looking at different parameters that allows the software to place you at the most likely nearby location in the database. The technology allows Foursquare to know much more about their users' habits, without them having to do much on their own. One of the new sources of revenue for

below left and right: Comme[n] tips and ratings can be added to places located with the Foursquare app.

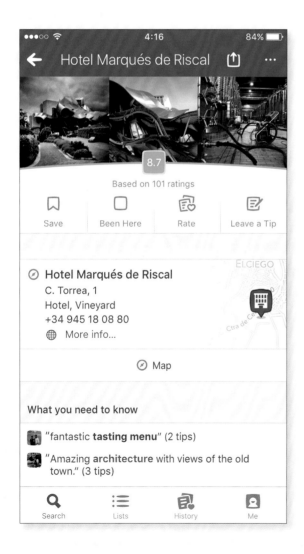

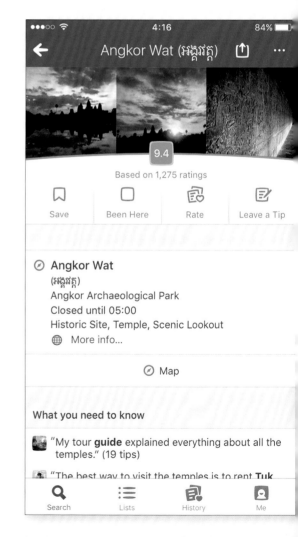

Foursquare, thanks to Pilgrim, is a classic Big Data product: predictions. In September 2015, Foursquare successfully predicted that Apple would sell between 13 and 15 million iPhone 6Ss on its first weekend of sales, by looking at the foot traffic in Apple stores. More recently, it correctly correlated a decline in foot traffic at the stores of fast-food chain Chipotle with a decline in sales, with a margin of error of less than 1 per cent.

Whose Data Is It?

It is highly likely that in the immense mountains of hyperlocal data generated in the last decade reside valuable insights about our cities and their problems, thanks to the active involvement of millions of citizens. Since 2009 the millions of annotations attached to objects in thousands of cities have created a new resource for urban intelligence that potentially opens up new forms of studying the evolution of cities. After Foursquare and the accumulation of hyperlocal data, urbanists, city planners and ethnographers could have a new lens to study the intricacies and potentially missed features of the urban fabric. The work of organisations such as the Center for Spatial Research at the Graduate School of Architecture, Planning and Preservation (GSAPP), Columbia University, New York, led by Laura Kurgan (see pages 72–7 of this issue), is pointing in interesting directions.

But the potential uses and the possibilities of including citizen-produced hyperlocal data in the new toolset for understanding cities is determined by the ownership and right of use of the data. As in many other cases, voluntary citizen-driven generation of data is happening within the enclosure of service-led businesses that are exploiting it commercially, but not bound to any other objective. Who owns this hyperlocal data? Who will preserve it? Who gets to use it, and in benefit of whom? These are, as always, the crucial questions that need to be addressed. ⌀

Geolocal apps are a resource for urban intelligence, opening up new means of studying the evolution of cities.

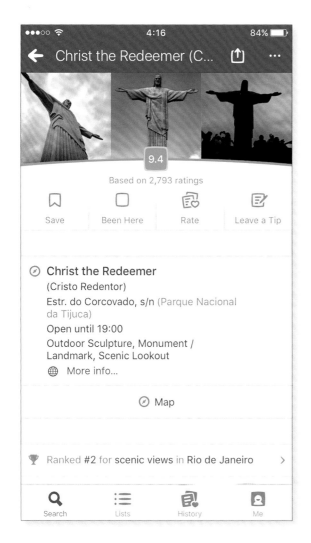

Who owns this hyperlocal data?

Who will preserve it?

Who gets to use it, and in benefit of whom?

Tell 'Em They're Dreamin'

COUNTERPOINT 01/2017 № 245 ⚠D

Mark Burry

Could 4D hyperlocal activism be the ultimate tool for popular resistance? This Counterpoint's title quotes the response of the main protagonist in Rob Sitch's 1997 film *The Castle* to developers' attempts at the compulsory purchase of his home. His act of refusal follows on from the decades-earlier writings of Herbert Marcuse and Ralph Adams Cram on the perils of capitalism and how they might be overcome. With reference to these, **Mark Burry**, a practising architect and Professor of Urban Futures at the University of Melbourne, considers the impact of technological enfranchisement on liveability.

Melbourne and its
rampant suburban
sprawl. Individual houses
cover almost the whole
of their plots in locations
far from the Central
Business District (CBD) or
any other concentrations
of employment.
Infrastructure is usually
provided post factum
in reaction to otherwise
predictable outcomes.

4D Hyperlocal encapsulates and catalogues a work in progress. The take-up of emerging technologies is fast moving and wide ranging, and potentially affords the end-user far greater engagement in urban planning and design than hitherto possible. The application of 4D hyperlocal strategies can be at any scale, too. Indeed, hyperlocal ranges from the smallest socially cohesive unit to the scale of the megacity: it all depends on context.

According to Guest-Editor Lucy Bullivant, '4D' in the title of this issue of ⟁ refers to the digital basis through which data is transacted, 'made possible by geolocation technologies and GPS-enabled mobile devices that support connectivity through open-source applications' (back cover). The volume is very much a future gaze that vigorously insinuates opportunities for boosting community engagement with the big decisions that affect them, made possible by harnessing more democratically managed technology. The collected essays propose various distinctive takes on 4D hyperlocal – essentially remote sensing, data collection and sharing, and participation in the decisions that immediately affect the community concerned. Combining these with design computation offers a complete rethink of how we design and organise our future cities, towns and villages, pervasively linked to citizen-operated frameworks attuned to singularly local circumstances and contexts.

Inevitably, hyperlocal will mean completely different things to different people depending on who they are, where they live, what they do and, absolutely crucially, what gets done to them. Here is my take on hyperlocal, writing from Melbourne, Australia, apparently the 'world's most liveable city' for the sixth year in a row at the time of writing.[1]

Hyperlocal Liveability

Melbourne is a medium-sized city of 4 million, but growing so rapidly that it is expected to have doubled in population by 2050. The 'world's most liveable city' honour comes from the Economist Intelligence Unit's *Global Liveability Ranking 2016*, leading to their annual *Most Liveable Cities Index*, drawn from their assessment of the same 140 major cities across the globe. The ranking can be compared to the allegedly less Anglo-centric *Mercer Quality of Living Survey*,[2] which compares 221

Inner suburban
Melbourne,
day and night,
2016

left top and bottom: The quaint
Victorian and Edwardian terraces
front a permanently kinetic
backdrop of non-stop construction.
4D hyperlocal gives citizens a
much better understanding of
what forces are at work, and some
new means to resist them.

Eastern fringe of
the Melbourne Central
Business District,
2002 and 2016

right and opposite left: Anticipated
to double in population to
8 million by 2050, the city
sprawls laterally accompanied
by a massive surge in inner-
city apartment tower-block
construction soaring in some
cases to over 60 floors. The 'boom'
is being fuelled significantly
by foreign speculators, and
not necessarily intended for
immediate occupation.

cities using 39 criteria. New York City is given a benchmark of 100 points against which the other 220 cities are rated in comparison. 'Liveability' is determined by citizens' relative access to life's practicalities and essentials such as high-quality education, health, cultural activity, transport and open space, all of which are tempered by perceived levels of risk from political tensions, terrorism or civil strife.

Unbelievably, liveability indices are driven solely by the need to determine levels of financial compensation for executives moving away from home to a city somewhere else, possibly on a different continent: the enforced stint of home away from home. The indices do not seem to consider the granularity, peculiarity or liveliness of the cities being measured: the *joie de vivre* and *je ne sais quoi*, for example, that may or may not give a city its real charm on an experiential scale. Cities like New York, Barcelona and London are relatively low in the indices despite, or perhaps because of, their edginess that many find so attractive. Nor do such indices even begin to touch upon the urban experiences of the cities' dispossessed, marginalised and abjectly less well-off cohabitees who are present to some extent either inconveniently conspicuously in the midst of the more well-to-do, or consigned to the periphery out of sight and out of mind – unless, of course, the underclass is sufficiently proportioned to undermine liveability standards for transient professional city dwellers.

The obstacles preventing clear, farsighted and rational yet poetic visions of desirable urban futures in Melbourne are the same as everywhere else I imagine – nimbyism, short-term political expediency, the lack of far-reaching planning frameworks and, most insidious of all, a lack of real ownership of the problem (or opportunity). It is hardly surprising that 'hyperlocalism' is a beacon signalling a potential role reversal to help fuel a counterculture

which, dare we dream it, subverts mainstream political ideologies and the hidden unelected hands of the corporate decision-makers, along with their supporting mainstream media. Certainly, if we the citizens could enjoy equal access to dwellings that are conducive to a shared sense of wellbeing, *civitas* could be the true credential of a successful city, and not merely its liveability.

Hyperlocal Activism

It is tempting to digress on this point. One could look at the decline of the Roman Empire, for example, and while not suggesting that its cities had all the virtues of equality, at least we could reflect anew on the Roman love of frameworks, and their visionary capacity that seems somewhat alien to today's decision-makers. There is no opportunity here either to deconstruct Thomas More's *Utopia* (1516)[3] alas, but even this most cursory reference draws attention to the role that 4D hyperlocal activism could play in advancing More's cause half a millennium later.

Although I am resisting being further sidetracked by informatively examining the potential for hyperlocal collectivism to be a more politically acceptable stage double for anarchy, we can usefully look at Herbert Marcuse's *One-Dimensional Man* (sic) for crumbs of 4D hyperlocal comfort[4] in passing. In this highly influential but ultimately self-defeating 1964 major work, Marcuse cites both contemporary capitalism and Soviet communism as being both equally latterday forms of social repression. As industrial society advances, regardless of either capitalist or communist political philosophy, he argued, both political persuasions, as systems, pursued the creation of false needs to boost industrial production, and with it the unsustainable levels of consumption disgracefully stimulated by mass media endorsement and advertising. The resulting one-dimensional universe of thought and behaviour behind

Ultimately, why, in the fullness of time, do such thoughtful critics of capitalism's relentlessly negative forces as Cram and Marcuse disappear so completely from view? How will future 4D *hyperlocalistes* avoid trending towards a similar fate?

File   Edit   View   Tools   Add   Help

Tour Guide   2012

the book's title has the intended effect of dulling critical thought and the human propensity to otherwise oppose the silent controlling forces typified by corporate behaviours. In promoting the 'great refusal'[5] as a means to shed the invisible shackles, could Marcuse's incitement of 'negative thinking'[6] to counter the positivist zeitgeist be reactivated through 4D hyperlocal activism?

Other historical figures such as the great architect and architectural scholar Ralph Adams Cram evinced similar political philosophies, though hardly so dense as Marcuse's. In reacting to the First World War, Cram published *Towards the Great Peace* in 1922.[7] Chapter 4 is titled 'The Industrial Problem' and presages many of the thoughts permeating Marcuse's oeuvre. While Cram did not espouse any particular path to activism to fly in the face of established political structures, he nevertheless attacked the motivations for, and effects of, industrialisation, holding back few punches in doing so. His sentiments

Public 4D hyperlocal at work: Marcus White, Notating pedestrian comfort in inner suburban North Melbourne, University of Melbourne, 2016

Diagramming the ease and timing for walkable access within an inner-city Melbourne primary school catchment. The school entrances are marked as yellow spheres, and the more intensely coloured blue spheres represent both favourable proximity and less direct exposure to sun. Such 4D hyperlocal tools based on publicly available information can inadvertently distort property prices as immediate locality advantages are exposed that were hitherto less obvious.

on the perils of capitalism and the loss of the 'joy' of labour (argued in Christian terms, it has to be noted) also foresee the driving instincts in many of the 4D hyperlocal contributions to this issue of △, such as those of Adam Greenfield, Alejandro Zaera-Polo, Martijn de Waal *et al* and Usman Haque.

Ultimately, why, in the fullness of time, do such thoughtful critics of capitalism's relentlessly negative forces as Cram and Marcuse disappear so completely from view? How will future 4D *hyperlocalistes* avoid trending towards a similar fate?

Celebrating the prescient *One-Dimensional Man* in the *Boston Review* 50 years after its publication, Ronald Aronson assessed Marcuse's failings thus: 'Marcuse didn't look for unexpected places where the system's contradictions might break out. He seemed to have too much faith in domination and too little in resistance, too much respect for the rulers and too little for the ruled.'[8] In terms of any grand ambitions for 4D hyperlocalism, the following passage from Aronson's half-century retrospective offers a significant cold shower with which to temper any blind faith:

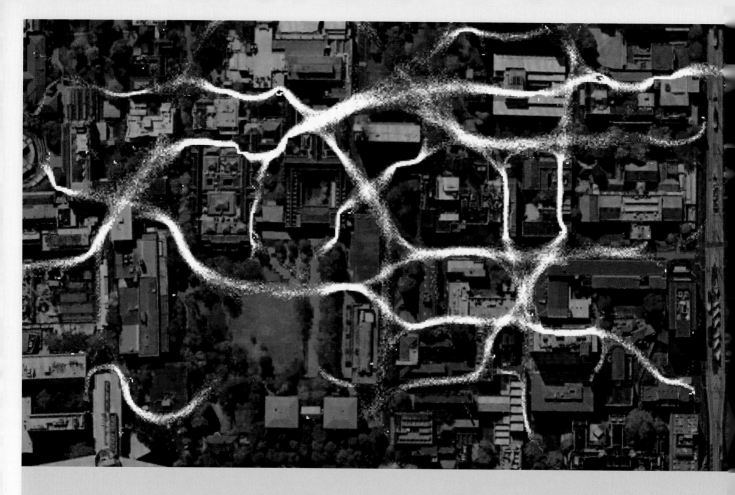

Private 4D hyperlocal at work: Gideon Aschwanden, Revealing pedestrian movement density, Melbourne Carlton Campus, University of Melbourne, 2016

above: Institutions such as the university depicted here can aggregate data from WiFi clients demonstrating the density of 10,000 simulated students on a campus moving between lectures. This dynamic 4D hyperlocal information is drawn from transient unique WiFi addresses, and can be used for any purpose unbeknownst to the people contributing the data.

Rob Sitch (director), *The Castle*, film still, 1997

below: In this scene from the film written, situated and produced in Melbourne, its chief protagonist Darryl Kerrigan is at home in the family's rather ordinary house, one that cannot have a price put on it. This witty film follows Darryl moving mountains to protect it from demolition. Is 'home as castle' the ultimate base-level definition of a functional 4D hyperlocal connected community?

Notes

1. Economist Intelligence Unit (EIU), *Global Liveability Ranking 2016*: www.eiu.com/public/topical_report.aspx?campaignid=liveability2016.
2. www.imercer.com/content/mobility/quality-of-living-city-rankings.html.
3. Thomas More, *Utopia* [1516], trans D Baker-Smith, Penguin Classics (London), 2012.
4. Herbert Marcuse, *One-Dimensional Man: Studies in the Ideology of Advanced Industrial Society*, Kindle edition: https://kindle.amazon.com/work/one-dimensional-man-ideology-industrial-routledge-ebook/B009T6YYJE/B00FVTSFRA.
5. 'Whether ritualized or not, art contains the rationality of negation. In its advanced positions, it is the Great Refusal – the protest against that which is.' Marcuse, *op cit*, p 66.
6. 'Such a critical standpoint [referring to that expressed by Marcuse] requires developing what Marcuse calls "negative thinking," which "negates" existing forms of thought and reality from the perspective of higher possibilities.' Douglas Kellner, 'Introduction to the Second Edition', in Marcuse, *op cit*, Location 106.
7. Ralph Adams Cram, *Towards the Great Peace*, Marshall Jones Company (Boston, MA), 1922.
8. Ronald Aronson, 'Marcuse Today', *Boston Review*, 17 November 2014: https://bostonreview.net/books-ideas/ronald-aronson-herbert-marcuse-one-dimensional-man-today.
9. *Ibid.*
10. The mini-series *Heimat* (11 episodes), televised in 1984, 'tells the story of the village Schabbach, on the Hunsrueck in Germany through the years 1919–1982'. It was followed in later years by two more series. See www.imdb.com/title/tt0087400/plotsummary?ref_=tt_ov_pl.
11. Quote from *The Castle*, directed by Rob Stich, Melbourne: Village Roadshow, 1997.
12. *Ibid.*
13. Luke Buckminster, 'The Castle: Rewatching Classic Australian Films', *The Guardian*, 4 April 2014: www.theguardian.com/film/australia-culture-blog/2014/apr/04/the-castle-rewatching-classic-australian-films.
14. Stephen Holden, 'Film Review: A Rhinestone That's Worth Fighting For', *The New York Times*, 7 May 1999: www.nytimes.com/1999/05/07/movies/film-review-a-rhinestone-that-s-worth-fighting-for.html.

The financial meltdown and Great Recession produced Occupy and indignados, but six years later the world system is unchanged, the culprits have escaped prosecution and, however bizarre it seems, the Tea Party sprang to life by demanding more of the same policies that caused the crisis in the first place.[9]

The Hyperlocality of Home

An antidote to thinking big yet failing through a naive overreach might be keeping hyperlocal very local, drawing on the lessons of 'the home' (in all its manifestations) as the minimum hyperlocal social unit. Associating 'home' with 'hyperlocal' is plausible as a lingua franca with which to extend this volume of ◬'s authors' varied – but in the main highly specific – accounts from their particular domains and circumstances into readers' own. But the transnational hyperlocal dialogue is transfused with linguistic nuance that can defeat a sense of a common language, if not a common cause; the cultural deficiencies that come from being locked within one's own language only adequately reveal themselves when another language is learned. The native Anglophone, for instance, will struggle to find the English equivalent for the German '*Heimat*'. Loosely translated as 'homeland', it carries far more nuance for the German sufferer, evoking in them a profound but displaced human connection with a distant geographical (spatial-social) unit such as the home village and its immediate environment from whence that individual has sprung, possibly a physical connection rescinded some time ago, and which is acutely missed.[10] Non-Galician-speaking Anglophones might care to look up '*morriña*' to feel another culture's sense of loss expressed in a single simple, phonetically expressive word that eludes the English language.

For the Spanish speaker, 'house' and 'home' is the same word – '*casa*' – thereby demanding subtleties of terminology not required in all languages. Regardless of how elusive the word 'home' might be in some cultures, sentimentally 'home is home' for everyone and, returning to Melbourne, in the case of Rob Sitch's classic 1997 Australian film *The Castle*, 'home as castle' is the core message. The plot is disarmingly simple: Darryl Kerrigan and family live in a very ordinary outer-suburban residence in Melbourne threatened by a compulsory purchase order for the house to be demolished to make way for an extension to the airport runway, onto which the house site backs. Their home is laden with the type of tacky souvenirs seen in ugly profusion at major tourist destinations, but elevated to an extraordinarily high status of treasured objectivised memories inside the Kerrigan household. The unprepossessing sponge cake and rissoles prepared by Darryl's wife with monotonous regularity are consistently met by the family with gleeful delight as an unexpected and exceptional culinary tour de force. The film's plot essentially details Darryl's fight to protect his home in a hilarious escalation of court battles, all the time making cute reference to successful epic struggles for the rights of Australia's traditional landowners.

Despite criticism of the film apparently sneering at lower-middle-class values, it carries a deceptively powerful message of 'the value of small gestures, assuming the best in people, picking your fights and being fiercely loyal to those you love'.[11] Darryl's refusal to accept the generous compensation package with 'You can't buy what I've got'[12] captures the film's essential universal spirit. It is witty throughout, and full of one-liners that have permanently joined the colourful and expressive uniquely Australian lexicon, such as Darryl's emphatically negative Marcusian response to the authorities' demands: 'Tell 'em they're dreamin'.'[13]

Darryl is deliberately presented as a one-dimensional character – in the theatrical sense, but also in Marcuse's sense of refusing to be the system's victim. It is an intelligently critical ode highlighting domestic ordinariness as a deceptive mask to the exceptional community instincts that a home such as that portrayed in *The Castle* represents: 'a storehouse of golden memories', one that should not be lightly given up.[14] 4D hyperlocal might be the most effective platform yet for the struggle against the top-down imposition of everything that compromises the rights of individuals to participate in a collective expression of a self-governing community's collective desires. Let us hope that 'the authorities' quickly appreciate that a technologically enfranchised vox populi will rapidly become a refusal to be reckoned with. ◬

CONTRIBUTORS

 ARCHITECTURAL DESIGN

4D HYPERLOCAL

Saskia Beer is a Dutch architect and urban entrepreneur, and founder of ZO!City and TransformCity®. She worked for offices in the Netherlands and Japan before later redefining her role through unsolicited local initiatives. In 2010 she acquired a stipend from the Dutch BKVB Fund and started Glamourmanifest (retitled ZO!City in 2015) to bring about bottom-up transformation of the Amstel3 business district of Amsterdam. She gives talks for students and professionals, has been a guest lecturer for the University of Amsterdam, Delft University of Technology (TU Delft) and the French educational urban planning institute IHEDATE, and regularly takes part in urban award juries.

Moritz Behrens is an architect and maker, an interaction designer and researcher trained at the Bartlett School of Architecture, University College London (UCL). He aims to combine architecture with human–computer interaction, focusing on designing for technology-mediated behaviours in public spaces, which encourage citizens and communities to engage with each other. He frequently speaks at conferences and his interactive installations have been exhibited at Verve Cultural in São Paulo, the EU-funded Connecting Cities Network, the Ars Electronica festival, and Vivid Sydney 2016. He recently received the Media Architecture Award 2016 in the Participatory Design and Urban Interaction category for his Sentiment Cocoon project.

John Bingham-Hall conducts research into culture and communication in the urban public, via interests such as urban soundscape, public art and hyperlocal media. He has degrees in music (Goldsmiths, University of London) and advanced architectural studies (Bartlett, UCL), and is currently completing a PhD in architectural space and computation at the Bartlett. He is researcher for Theatrum Mundi, a network of artists and urbanists based at LSE Cities at the London School of Economics in London concerned with the conditions of cultural production in the city. Outside of academia he has worked on meanwhile use projects with the Architecture Foundation, Argent and Bistrotheque, and undertakes consulting on urban culture.

Matthijs Bouw is a Dutch architect and urbanist, and founder of One Architecture (established in 1995), an award-winning Amsterdam- and New York-based design and planning firm. He is the Rockefeller Urban Resilience Fellow for PennDesign at the University of Pennsylvania. In New York City, the office is currently part of a multidisciplinary team executing the first phase of the East Side Coastal Resiliency scheme for Lower Manhattan, as well as planning the Lower Manhattan Coastal Protection project. In the Netherlands, One Architecture is part of the Hackable City team for Buiksloterham, a large-scale brownfield redevelopment based on the principles of the circular economy.

Mark Burry is a practising architect, and has principally published on the life and work of Antoni Gaudí, and on putting theory into practice with 'challenging' architecture. He is Senior Architect to the Sagrada Família Basilica Foundation, pioneering distant design collaboration with his Barcelona colleagues. In December 2014 he joined the University of Melbourne as Professor of Urban Futures at the Faculty of Architecture, Building and Planning, where he helps consolidate the faculty's research capacity in urban futures, drawing together expertise in urban visualisation, analytics and policy. Prior to this appointment, he was the Founding Director of RMIT University's Design Research Institute (DRI), and also founded the university's state-of-the-art Spatial Information Architecture Laboratory (SIAL) in 2001.

Will Gowland is a London-based architect, maker and spatial animator. On graduating from the Architectural Association (AA) in London with the prestigious Baylight Scholarship in 2013, he cofounded UniversalAssemblyUnit with Samantha Lee, a multidisciplinary design studio working at the intersection of art, technology and culture. His interests lie in the emerging field of design interactions and in the exploration of spatial design and virtual environments through audiovisual performance, physical installations and animation.

Adam Greenfield lives in London. His next book, *Radical Technologies: The Design of Everyday Life*, is forthcoming from Verso.

Usman Haque is a founding partner of Umbrellium and Thingful, a search engine for the Internet of Things. Prior to this he launched the Internet of Things data infrastructure and community platform Pachube.com. Trained as an architect, he has created responsive environments, interactive installations, digital interface devices and dozens of mass-participation initiatives throughout the world. He has also taught at the Bartlett School of Architecture, UCL, including the Interactive Architecture Workshop (until 2005), and is currently co-teaching the RC12 Urban Design cluster 'Participatory Systems for Networked Urban Environments'. In 2008 he received the Design of the Year Award (interactive) from the Design Museum, London.

Agustin Indaco is a PhD candidate in economics at the Graduate Center, City University of New York (CUNY). He was a researcher for the World Bank between 2010 and 2012 and an adjunct professor at New York City College of Technology. He is currently a member of the Software Studies Lab at the University of California, San Diego and the Graduate Center, CUNY, working on analysis of social media shared in cities, and a columnist for *El Economista* (Argentina).

Bess Krietemeyer is a designer and researcher, currently a Syracuse Center of Excellence (SyracuseCoE) Faculty Fellow and Assistant Professor at the Syracuse University School of Architecture. Her expertise lies at the intersection of sustainable architectural technologies, interactive systems and performance simulation. She holds a PhD in architectural sciences from the Center for Architecture Science and Ecology (CASE) at Rensselaer Polytechnic Institute, New York, and has practised professionally on international projects that incorporate next-generation building systems. She leads the Interactive Design and Visualization Lab at SyracuseCoE, where her research focuses on hybrid-reality simulations for interactive design and energy analysis.

Laura Kurgan is an Associate Professor of Architecture at the Graduate School of Architecture, Planning and Preservation (GSAPP) at Columbia University, New York, where she directs the Visual Studies curriculum and the Center for Spatial Research (formerly the Spatial Information Design Lab, which she founded in 2004). She is the author of *Close Up at a Distance: Mapping, Technology, and Politics* (Zone Books, 2013). Her work ranges from explorations of digital mapping technologies to the ethics and politics of mapping, and the art, science and visualisation of data. Her work has appeared at the Cartier Foundation in Paris, Venice Architecture Biennale, Barcelona Museum of Contemporary Art, ZKM|Center for Art and Media Karlsruhe, and the Museum of Modern Art (MoMA), New York.

Michiel de Lange is an Assistant Professor in New Media Studies in the Department of Media and Culture Studies at Utrecht University, where he currently heads the Media and Culture Studies Expertise Centre, a public lab that engages in collaborations and partnerships with the professional media and culture field. He obtained a PhD in philosophy (2010) from the Erasmus University Rotterdam, and works as a researcher and lecturer in (mobile) media, urban culture, identity and play. He is the cofounder (with Martijn de Waal) of the Mobile City, a platform for the study of new media and urbanism.

Samantha Lee is a media artist based in London. She has an architecture degree from the Architectural Association in London from where she graduated in 2012, when she was nominated for Diploma Honours and featured in Blueprint Magazine's 'Best Graduates of 2012.' In 2013 with architect Will Gowland she cofounded UniversalAssemblyUnit, a multidisciplinary design studio using digital technologies to create new behaviours, concepts and form. Having previously worked at 3D scanning company ScanLAB, she continues her interest in 3D digital capture as photographic technique, creating images and video work to express abstract materiality and virtual landscapes.

Lev Manovich is a Professor at The Graduate Center, CUNY and a Director of the Software Studies Lab at the University of California, San Diego and the Graduate Center, CUNY that uses data science to study cultures. The Lab's recent projects were commissioned by MoMA, New York Public Library, and Google. He appeared on the list of '25 People Shaping the Future of Design' (Complex.com) in 2013 and among the '50 Most Interesting People Building the Future' (The Verge) in 2014. Manovich is author and editor of eight books including *Data Drift: Archiving Media and Data Art in the 21st Century* (RIXC LieP MP Lab, 2015), *Software Takes Command* (Bloomsbury, 2013), *Soft Cinema: Navigating the Database* (with Andreas Kratky, MIT Press, 2005) and *The Language of New Media* (MIT Press, 2001).

Claudia Pasquero is cofounder and director of ecoLogicStudio in London, director of the Urban Morphogenesis Lab at the Bartlett School of Architecture, UCL, and a member of the senior teaching faculty at the Institute for Advanced Architecture of Catalonia (IAAC) in Barcelona. She is also an ADAPT-r Research Fellow, investigating the cultural relevance of bio-computation at the Department of Architecture and Urban Design, Estonian Academy of Arts in Tallinn. She holds a degree in engineering from Turin Polytechnic and an MA from the AA in London. She has been a studio master at the AA and at Cornell University, New York. Her work has been exhibited at the Venice Architecture Biennale, and is part of collections include FRAC in Orléans, France, and ZKM|Karlsruhe.

Marco Poletto is an architect, author and educator. He is cofounder and director of ecoLogicStudio in London, and currently holds an ADAPT-r Research Fellowship in biodigital design at the Aarhus School of Architecture, Denmark. He is Distinguished Visiting Critic at Carnegie Mellon University in Pittsburgh, Pennsylvania. After graduating with Honours from Turin Polytechnic, he moved to London to study at the AA. He has lectured and taught internationally, has been a unit master at the AA and the Bartlett School of Architecture, UCL, and is a member of the Visiting Faculty at the IAAC, Barcelona, and Cornell University. He is co-author, with Claudia Pasquero, of *Systemic Architecture: Operating Manual for the Self-Organizing City* (Routledge, 2012).

Raffaele Pe focuses his research on interactive cartography, immersive landscapes, and space design across new media. He received his PhD in architectural studies in 2014, following his graduation from the Polytechnic University of Milan in 2009 (where he is currently a contract professor in spatial design and composition), a second degree at Turin Polytechnic, and a Diploma in Innovation Processes at the Alta Scuola Politecnica in Italy. In 2012 he became a visiting PhD researcher at the Royal College of Art, London, and since May 2014 has been a Fellow of the Cini Foundation, Venice. He is the author of *Spazi Aurali: Architettura e Sound Design* (Postmedia Books, 2016), and *Agogic Maps* (Springer, forthcoming).

José Luis de Vicente is a curator and cultural researcher. He develops projects at the intersection of culture, technology and design. He is the curator for 'Sónar+D', the Creative Technologies section of Barcelona's acclaimed Sonar Festival, as well as the Futureeverything festival in Manchester, UK. He runs the Visualizar Programme for Data Culture at Medialab Prado, Madrid. His most recent exhibition is 'Big Bang Data' (Centre de Cultura Contemporània de Barcelona, Fundació Telefónica Madrid and Somerset House, London). He teaches at the IAAC Barcelona.

Martijn de Waal is a senior researcher in the lectorate of Play & Civic Media, Amsterdam University of Applied Sciences. He is the author of *The City as Interface: How Digital Media Are Changing the City* (nai010 Publishers, 2014). He is a cofounder of the Mobile City Foundation, an international research group that explores the relationship between digital media and urban culture through workshops, conferences and publications. He is currently the project leader of the Hackable City research project, a collaboration between the University of Amsterdam, the Amsterdam University of Applied Sciences, Utrecht University and One Architecture. The project is funded by the Netherlands Organisation for Scientific Research.

Katharine Willis is Associate Professor (Reader) in Digital Environments at the School of Art, Design and Architecture at Plymouth University, UK. Her research over the last decade has explored the effects and implications of digital networks on the experience and design of urban space and place. She has authored and edited over 40 publications on these themes. Recent books include *Netspaces: Space and Place in a Networked World* (Routledge, 2016), *Locative Media: Multidisciplinary Perspectives on Media and Locality* (Transcript Press, 2013) and *Shared Encounters* (Springer, 2010).

Alejandro Zaera-Polo is a contemporary architect, and the founder of Foreign Office Architects/FOA (1993) and AZPML (2011). He trained at the Escuela Técnica Superior de Arquitectura de Madrid, and the Harvard University Graduate School of Design (GSD). Prior to establishing FOA, he worked at OMA in Rotterdam between 1991 and 1993. He is the author of *The Sniper's Log: Architectural Chronicles of Generation X* (Actar, 2013), and has been published in magazines such as *El Croquis, Quaderns, A+U, Arch+, Log, Δ* and *Harvard Design Magazine*. He is a Professor at the Princeton School of Architecture, New Jersey, and has taught at the Berlage Institute in Rotterdam, Yale University School of Architecture, the AA, Columbia GSAPP and the University of California, Los Angeles (UCLA) School of Architecture.

What is Architectural Design?

Founded in 1930, *Architectural Design* (Δ) is an influential and prestigious publication. It combines the currency and topicality of a newsstand journal with the rigour and production qualities of a book. With an almost unrivalled reputation worldwide, it is consistently at the forefront of cultural thought and design.

Each title of Δ is edited by an invited Guest-Editor, who is an international expert in the field. Renowned for being at the leading edge of design and new technologies, Δ also covers themes as diverse as architectural history, the environment, interior design, landscape architecture and urban design.

Provocative and inspirational, Δ inspires theoretical, creative and technological advances. It questions the outcome of technical innovations as well as the far-reaching social, cultural and environmental challenges that present themselves today.

For further information on Δ, subscriptions and purchasing single issues see:

www.architectural-design-magazine.com

How to Subscribe
With 6 issues a year, you can subscribe to Δ (either print, online or through the Δ App for iPad)

Institutional subscription
£275 / US$516
print or online

Institutional subscription
£330 / US$620
combined print and online

Personal-rate subscription
£128 / US$201
print and iPad access

Student-rate subscription
£84 / US$129
print only

Δ App for iPad
6-issue subscription:
£44.99 / US$64.99
Individual issue:
£9.99 / US$13.99

To subscribe to print or online
E: cs-journals@wiley.com

Americas
E: cs-journals@wiley.com
T: +1 781 388 8598
or +1 800 835 6770
(toll free in the USA & Canada)

Europe, Middle East and Africa
E: cs-journals@wiley.com
T: +44 (0) 1865 778315

Asia Pacific
E: cs-journals@wiley.com
T: +65 6511 8000

Japan (for Japanese-speaking support)
E: cs-japan@wiley.com
T: +65 6511 8010
or 005 316 50 480
(toll-free)

Visit our Online Customer Help available in 7 languages at www.wileycustomerhelp.com/ask

Volume 86 No 1
ISBN 978 1118 910641

Volume 86 No 2
ISBN 978 1118 736166

Volume 86 No 3
ISBN 978 1118 972465

Volume 86 No 4
ISBN 978 1118 951057

Volume 86 No 5
ISBN 978 1118 954980

Volume 86 No 6
ISBN 978 1119 099581